# CAN GOD
# CREATE
# A ROCK
## SO BIG
## HE CAN'T
## MOVE IT?

# CAN GOD CREATE A ROCK

## SO BIG HE CAN'T MOVE IT?

### DAREK ISAACS

Alachua, Florida 32615

**Bridge-Logos**
Alachua, FL 32615 USA

*Can God Create A Rock So Big He Can't Move It?*
by Darek Isaacs

Copyright ©2012 by Bridge-Logos

Edited by Harold J. Chadwick

Printed in the United States of America.

Library of Congress Catalog Card Number: 2012940609
International Standard Book Number: 978-0-88270-475-3

# DEDICATION

◆ ◆ ◆

*For my daughter, Evelyn*

# TABLE OF CONTENTS

◆ ◆ ◆

# PREFACE

◆ ◆ ◆

The modern church has melded into the world. We look like the world, we talk like the world, and we get entertained as the world. Our salt and light have become bland and dim. Even worse, many from the pulpit have adopted secular views on things as wide as our origins, our endings, the meaning of marriage, and even our ways of leadership. And the results of these compromises have led to an avalanche within the church, which is only building momentum.

We see the rise of the emergent church. We see the rise of new-age spiritualism within the church. We see the rise of religious universalism. Most shockingly, we see the rise of replacement theology, which is a full hijacking of the very heritage and mission of the Jewish Messiah and, therefore, the Bible itself. These are all failures that fracture the health of the believer and discombobulate the unified and simple message of Messiah.

What is quite alarming is the sheer volume of the heresies, and the rate at which they are coming. The mind of the modern human seems to have been conditioned to be the most fertile soil to any new idea that wishes to change, augment, adapt, and allegorize any and every part of Scripture. We have become completely Greek in our way of thinking, something our Messiah never was.

These ideas have consequences in our lives. We witness within the so-called church that the actions of most of the pew-dwellers are no different than the actions within the society that so openly rejects God. It is obvious that we have prostituted the purity of the bride as we clamor for the attention and respect of the secular world.

This has happened because we somehow

figured that a water-pistol delivery of the gospel is somehow more effective than bringing the full rising of the tide. We have been duped into believing that presenting a partial truth is somehow more effective than the total truth. We have believed this lie because we have believed that the faith in which we stand is actually a bit blinder than what we had hoped.

Yet the opposite of that is true. The greatness of the Bible is stronger than what the mind of man can possibly comprehend. It is more cutting than a double-edged sword. But then, how did we get so confused? The answer is that Satan has commandeered our minds.

But I am here to say, it is time to take them back.

Remarkably enough, the pathway to winning back our minds is answering the age old paradox, "Can God create a rock so big He can't move it?"

# CHAPTER ONE

# THREE HOORAYS FOR JORGE!

◆ ◆ ◆

From rabbis to pastors to priests, we all know that a good parable or anecdote always finds its use. And as we are about to dive into what has been nicknamed the Rock Paradox, which is the age old question, "Can God create a rock so big He can't move it?", it dawned on me that we should take a page from the pulpit and start out with something a bit entertaining.

So, before we cannonball into deeper waters, let's first take a journey through time with a man named Jorge. As a disclaimer, you should know that what follows is a bit of a mindbender. It may make you feel like your brain is trying to tie a knot with a frozen rope. But what's the point of a riddle if it doesn't leave you riddled?

Exactly! You're off to a great start.

This tale begins a few centuries ago with an eccentric inventor named Jorge. Jorge had a reputation for being a bit of a recluse and not always up with the times.

In Jorge's younger years he traveled by boat from the coastline of South America, the region of his birth, until he landed in the New England colonies. Along the way, he gathered various leaves and herbs.

One day in an uneventful first week of July, Jorge was speaking to a watchmaker who had designed the most perfectly tuned stopwatch in the world. The only shortcoming of the stopwatch was that it would not measure time for more than

24 hours per session from the time it was initiated.

It recorded perfect time, up until 24 hours, and then it would completely stop on that terminal strike of the 24$^{th}$ hour. To begin the stopwatch again, the user had to first rewind the stopwatch to full strength.

As Jorge listened to the watchmaker, his eyes spread wide like saucers and he bought that unique watch that day.

Unbeknownst to the watchmaker, Jorge had been working on an invention—a secret liquid formula that he would soon use in an experiment. But the experiment needed a constant variable. This stopwatch provided that.

That same day, Jorge wrote duplicate letters to his two brothers who also left their homeland of South America in their youth. Andreas lived in England, and Eduardo lived in Italy.

Jorge wrote:

Andreas and Eduardo, my dear brothers!

This is your younger brother Jorge. I have made a formula from the herbs that I gathered from South America. In these herbs I have found the secret to time travel!

I am here to tell you, that on the day of our dear mother's birth I am going to travel into the future!

You are my witnesses, as is this letter.

Your brother, Jorge.

Jorge rushed to the dock and found a captain who claimed he had the fastest boat in the world. Jorge paid the captain to deliver these letters to his brothers in England and Italy.

Meanwhile, Jorge worked to perfect his formula, and he tied the stopwatch around his neck with a lanyard.

Weeks went by and it finally reached 5:00

in the afternoon of his mother's birthday. Jorge went upstairs to the attic where he kept all of his experiments and inventions. He poured his time travel formula into his favorite mug. He started the stopwatch and chugged the formula.

Within minutes, lights began dancing all around him, and then the lights started to sing to him! He stood at the top of the stairs and muttered, "The stairs go up and down, yet they never move!" and he chuckled.

Before his laugh ended, Jorge blacked out, and he did a face-first plummet down the stairs.

The stopwatch continued to keep perfect time.

Time passed and Jorge began to wake. As he lifted up his head, he felt the weight of the stopwatch around his neck, and he instantly sobered and jerked the face of the watch to within inches from his nose and looked at the dial.

The stopwatch was still ticking and it was just past 12 hours of time.

He bolted outside and rushed to the corner where the local newsboys sold their papers. He rushed at them and grabbed the first front page he could reach.

Jorge's eyes went straight to the date at the top of the paper. Jorge gasped "It's been almost two weeks since my mother's birthday!"

He sat down heavily and quickly on the side of the road and carefully replayed the events in his mind.

Approximately 12 hours ago he drank his time travel formula and began the stopwatch. That was the day of his mother's birthday. He soon passed out and fell down the stairs. When he awoke 12 hours later, he rushed to the newsboys who had today's paper, where he saw that nearly two weeks had passed since his mother's birthday.

Jorge stood up and yelled, "I have traveled into the future!"

**How Did This Happen?**
Here are the accounts of the brothers in England and Italy.

When the ship reached the coasts of England, the captain of the ship hired a local courier to finish the route and deliver the letter to Andreas while the ship then set sail to deliver the other letter to Eduardo in Italy.

However, the local carrier in England got lost and by the time he delivered the letter to Andreas in England, Eduardo had already received his letter nine days earlier in Italy.

But, Andreas received the letter 3 days before their mother's birthday, and Eduardo, received the letter the evening before their mother's birthday.

## How Did This Happen?

Three months later, Jorge received two letters from his brothers. The first was from Andreas. It read:

> My Brother!
>
> You have done it. Just as you said, you have altered time! On the day of our dear mother's birth, I celebrated your experiment with a grand party at my favorite pub in London. I made a toast, and the crowd gave you three mighty hoorays! I admit, I had a bit too much to drink and the night is more than a little hazy in my memory. However, when I did finally wake, I strolled into town to get the local paper, and nearly two weeks had passed since our dear mother's birthday! I had traveled with you into the future!
>
> Your Brother, Andreas

Jorge was enthralled. He had independent confirmation from his brother, Andreas, in England.

But there was another letter that came that day. Jorge saw it was from Italy and recognized the handwriting; it was from his oldest brother Eduardo:

My Dear Brother,

I admit, I was intrigued to fall asleep the night of our mother's birthday, but when I woke up the next morning, and it was simply the next day of the same week, I instantly felt sorry for you. I am sorry you failed

Your Brother, Eduardo

Jorge was beyond perplexed at the two totally different accounts of his two brothers.

**How Did This Happen?**
Three times, this riddle asks the question, "How did this happen?"

If you answer it correctly once, you answer it correctly all three times. All for one, and one for all.

**Bonus Question:** What was the date of their mother's birthday?

# CHAPTER TWO

# JORGE'S ANSWER

◆ ◆ ◆

In the year 46 B.C., the Julian calendar was developed and added Leap Year to provide a more accurate calendar. However, the Julian calendar was still imprecise.

In the year 1582, the Bishop of Rome, reformed the calendar, and what was known as the Gregorian calendar was adopted and it replaced the Julian calendar. The Gregorian calendar had to correct 1,600 years of imprecision caused by the Julian calendar.

However, the British and their colonies, which included the American colonies, did not convert from the Julian calendar to the Gregorian calendar until the year 1752. By that time, there were 11 days that had to be deleted due to the mistake of the Julian calendar.

George Washington was alive at this time and he went to bed on September 2nd, 1752, and September 3, 4, 5, 6, 7, 8, 9, 10, 11, 12, and 13 were all deleted (eleven days in all) and he woke up on September 14th, as did the rest of the British Empire.

In "Three Hoorays for Jorge," September 2nd was the birthday of the mother of the three brothers.

On September 2nd, 1752, Jorge, living in the colonies, drank a mixture from various plant extracts, which made him hallucinate. He then fell down the stairs, and became unconscious.

Jorge's Answer

He woke up 12 hours later, which was confirmed by the stopwatch. He then rushed outside and discovered the date. It was September 14th, 1752.

Andreas, who was in England, also passed out due to excessive alcohol on September 2nd, 1752 and when he awoke, it was September 14th, 1752.

Both Andreas and Jorge were victims of the calendar being changed, which accounted for their "time travel." Jorge, though he tried, was never able to repeat his experiment, to his great frustration.

Eduardo, who lived in Italy, was already living by the Gregorian calendar. When he went to bed on September 2nd he woke up on September 3rd.

However, Eduardo's September 2nd was different than both Andreas' and Jorge's September 2nd. When Eduardo celebrated their mother's birthday, it was still August 22nd for his two brothers. And When Jorge

25

and Andreas celebrated their Mothers birthday on their September 2$^{nd}$, it was September 13$^{th}$ in Italy where Eduardo was.

Eduardo's September 2$^{nd}$ was earlier than both Jorge's and Andreas' September 2$^{nd,}$ which accounts for him receiving the letter days before Andreas, but only the night before his mother's birthday. Whereas, Andreas received the letter after Eduardo received his, but he still had a few days to spare before his mother's birthday.

# CHAPTER THREE

# THE ROCK PARADOX

◆ ◆ ◆

"Three Hoorays for Jorge" offered a growing collection of facts that appeared to be in diametrical opposition. Yet, when all the information was discovered, what once appeared to be illogical rubble took the shape of an organized structure. The opening riddle demonstrated that once all the data is known even that which seems confusing at first glance can become very clear.

This brings us to the amazing question that has been called "The Rock Paradox," which is, "Can God create a rock so big He can't move it?"

In the preparation for writing this book, I asked many people this question and heard a wide swath of answers, but none were satisfactory. My favorite riposte, in terms of providing a wow factor, came from a college student who revealed to me that he had asked this same question of a theology professor. This was the answer the professor gave to him:

> "God can create a rock very large. And then God can lessen His own power so that He can no longer move the rock. But then, God can increase His own power so that He can move the rock He formerly could not."

If that is a professor of theology, then that is an indictment of western seminaries—for I am not sure one can find a bigger theological train wreck than what that answer was.

Here is another *answer* to the Rock Paradox that I will always remember:

> "We are confined to the dimensions that we live in. However, God is not. In another dimension, like a fourth dimension where perhaps heaven is, where the laws of nature are different, God can certainly do that there."

I give this one an A for effort, and an F for believability. The provider of this conclusion was guilty of pushing the answer to a place where no one could ever find it. Making an answer unreachable is not an answer.

The most common response to the question, "Can God create a rock so big He can't move it?" was this, "Yes. If God wanted to, God can do it, because He can do anything."

This very common answer of yes to the Rock Paradox based on the "God can do anything premise" fails—for if God does succeed in creating a rock He no longer can move, then the end result of creating the rock proves God cannot do absolutely everything because He is stuck staring at a rock He cannot move. Therefore, the end result falsifies the beginning assumption, which led to the answer of yes in the first place.

In the wake of this inescapable rock, some have decided to act like the question does not even exist.

A professor at my graduate school stated this:

> "Can God make a rock so heavy that He couldn't lift it? It's a rather silly question, isn't it? . . . Some questions are not worth the asking and certainly not worth the answering. So I wouldn't try."[1]

---

1    Liberty Professor, *Church History*, Liberty University

I did not like the spirit of this response. To me, it is not acceptable to claim the question is not worth the time, or to simply disregard it as irrelevant. If one does this, they risk insulting the person who asks it— for such an answer makes it seem as though the inquirer is not worth the time to be given a serious answer.

I think Augustine of Hippo stated it well when he said that spiritual questions deserved a serious effort. Even though Augustine is not referring to our Rock Paradox, the spirit of his response rings true in our case.

> "I don't answer facetiously, shrugging off the force of the question as a certain one is reported to have done. . . . I would've willingly answered, "I don't know what I don't know," instead of causing the one who asked a deep question to be ridiculed— especially if such tactics gain praise for a worthless answer."[2]

2   Augustine of Hippo, Confessions, Bridge Logos, 2003, pg. 320

None of us are the keepers of all knowledge. Simply because one person cannot offer an answer does not mean that a valid answer does not exist. We should not dismiss questions based on the criteria that the answer is elusive.

On a more serious note, a friend informed me of a missionary in China who was asked the Rock Paradox question as a challenge. When the missionary had no response, the Chinese man said, "If you can't answer that, then I have no time for your God."

An editor and founder of a magazine, whose sole purpose is to defend authority of Scripture, told me in a phone conversation that he would love to know the answer to the Rock Paradox because he has been asked it in a public forum and couldn't provide a suitable answer.

I attended an event at Jacksonville State University, where a Christian scholar was giving a public presentation about the veracity of Scripture. JSU is a secular university and a local church helped arrange the public session as an outreach event. At the end of the presentation there was a planned time to allow the scholar to field some questions from the audience.

However, the pastor, who helped arrange the event, was informed that a baseball player at the university was going to ask the Rock Paradox question. When he heard this, he cancelled the Q&A session!

Is this question really something that Bible believers have to dodge? Is it something that should be dismissed as silly and not worth the time to answer? I doubt the missionary, when faced with an unbelieving antagonist, found the question to be so irrelevant.

The very existence of the Rock Paradox actually causes another issue to surface. With so many Bible professors, apologists, missionaries, and pastors being uncomfortably faced with this challenge, is it possible that a mockery has been wrapped in riddle? And if this is the case, could the Rock Paradox be one of the most theologically important questions of all time?

1 Peter 3:15 teaches that those who believe in the Messiah should always be prepared to give an answer for the hope that we have in Him. And the Bible further teaches how to find this wisdom, understanding, and knowledge.

> [Yes], if you call out for insight and raise your voice for understanding, if you seek it like silver and search for it as for hidden treasures, then you will understand the fear of the LORD and find the knowledge of God. For the LORD gives wisdom; from his mouth come knowledge and understanding; (Proverbs 2:3-6)

Why has the Rock Paradox become so troublesome? Have we stopped seeking the Lord, or worse yet, have we lost reverence for the Lord? For such is the beginning of knowledge.

# CHAPTER FOUR

# THE GREATNESS OF GOD

◆ ◆ ◆

O ur life is a rapid sprint that never slows. In the limited time we are given, we should strive to be deeper developed with every stride. This is not something that *should* happen—it really *must* happen in all of us who are serious about responding to the call of Messiah with any intentionality.

Make no mistake; there is a charge and a mandate given to all of us to mature in our faith. We are to amplify the conviction of our commission and grow in wisdom, understanding, and knowledge. But many of us have opted to be stagnant in our faith. Instead of maturing, we are simply just aging.

To answer the challenge of the rock paradox with any kind of resolution, it will take a deeper effort to truly understand not only the meaning of our Bible, but the nature of the one and only God, who is the God of the Bible. This is something that I think the westernized church, which so desperately wants a user-friendly God, has failed to achieve.

Mercifully, it does not take a theological degree to understand God. Often degrees in theology only make things worse. The beauty of our faith is that the deepest profundities have been made understandable to any eager mind—to people just like you and me.

This is because Jesus the Christ (His true Jewish name is Yeshua) did not leave any of us alone. We have a comforter and instructor, who is the Holy Spirit who lives inside the believer. The profound truth in this matter is that we are not singular if we are born again—who I am is not only me.

As we study the Scripture to find an answer to our question, we must begin with the set parameters that the Bible is the divinely inspired Word of God and is profitable for all teaching. We also believe that it is accessible and understandable to the average person who has the desire to seek. Therefore, a literal reading is the best place to begin with understanding Scripture. We also acknowledge that we must have the discipline to dedicate ourselves in order to understand the historical context and references that are inherent within the Jewish context of all Scripture.

Now, we should not confuse a literal reading with a wooden reading. A literal reading can and should take into consideration language of phenomenon, hyperbole, and context. And a literal reading is meant to incorporate proper historical context so that the intent of the divine author can be ascertained.

As an example, when Jesus was speaking to His disciples during the Passover recorded in Luke 22, He most notably referred to His body as the bread and His blood as the wine that they were about to eat and drink (Luke 22:19-20). What was our Messiah's intent with such graphic language?

A wooden reading of the text would make one think that Christ was offering His flesh as the meal, or perhaps His body actually consisted of fermented grapes and baked flour. This, of course, was not the intent of our Lord. He was not promoting cannibalism.

Knowing the biblical context is critical to understanding the words of our Messiah. Jesus was connecting His Passover dinner with the disciples, to the historic Passover recorded in Exodus 12, which occurred when Israel was in bondage in Egypt.

In Egypt, each Jewish family was to take a lamb, which was without blemish, into their house on the 10th day of Nisan. The family was to keep the lamb for four days and then on the 14th, all of Israel was instructed to kill their lambs at twilight.

The people were to take some of the blood of the lamb and put it on the doorposts of the homes. This blood was a sign of their relationship with the Holy One of Israel, and because of that sign their families were spared from the disaster that came upon the Egyptians.

Then, the people of Israel were instructed to eat the entire lamb, and eat it with haste. This is why the Lord said the meal was His body and blood—for He was the Lamb of God that brought salvation from the judgment.

The Lord spoke in a way that the observant Jewish individual would understand. He demonstrated to all subsequent generations that His life, like the lambs in Egypt, would lead to the salvation of His people.

And like the Passover lambs of Egypt, on the 10th day of Nisan, Jesus was delivered, by the Lord's will, for the people of Israel and all other nations. He was on trial for four days and he was found to be without blemish—for Pilate found no guilt in Him. Jesus then became the guilt offering for the salvation of all, just as prophesied in Isaiah 53:10:

> [When] his soul makes an offering for guilt, he shall see his offspring; he shall prolong his days; the will of the LORD shall prosper in his hand.

The Lord Jesus laid down His life to save the lives of others.

Furthermore, God brought the twilight early the day of the crucifixion so the event of our Lord's death corresponded with the twilight death of the Passover lambs at the Passover in Egypt. Therefore, understanding the context illuminates the deeper meaning, and also allows one to avoid misunderstandings.

There is not a single author I know who would want a wooden interpretation of their work today. An ingredient to our humanity is that we use dynamic language to stress important points. This is simply how we were created. Such language aids in our retention of important matters. Therefore, it would make sense that our Creator would communicate to us in this way.

Why then is it that people are not understanding the Bible if it is given to us in an understandable fashion? Well, this question has a very easy answer I think —most people have never read the entire Bible.

If a person does not start in Genesis and end with Revelation, how can one really understand the overarching themes, the consistent threads, and the context of the whole? How can one understand what it means to be under grace, if they have no concept of the condemnation found under the law? How can one understand the role of the gentile believer, who is the wild branch grafted in, if they have no concept of the Jewish root into which they have been grafted? How can one understand the sacrificial system in Leviticus, if they don't understand its satisfaction and completion through the life, death, and resurrection of Jesus? They can't.

My point is, if we constantly treat the Bible like an á la carte offering by reading it in selective chunks, then we are going to miss the immersive experience. Our Messiah's intention was to give us a complete landscape portrait of His plan. However, many have opted for the picture of a kaleidoscope instead. In doing so, the reader misses the building themes and spiritual crescendos that become so relevant to understanding the whole biblical narrative.

Most Christians miss the extraordinary beauty when the themes of the Old Covenant are married with the completion of the New Covenant. Often, we never see the harmony of the two becoming one.

Obviously, an incomplete understanding of the biblical text is a liability and can be dangerous. In a very simplistic example, I will use Philippians 4:13 to demonstrate the error in taking something out of context: "I can do all things through him who strengthens me."

At face value, this is a very sweeping statement in the Bible. Does this verse mean that someone is justified to do all things and think that the strength of Christ justifies their actions? Of course not.

Christ does not give us the fortitude and resolve to murder, maim, and commit

45

atrocious acts of sin. There is a context implied in this verse. Paul was writing to the church in Philippi and was encouraging them that they can overcome hardships through complete dependency on Christ.

Furthermore, understanding the Ten Commandments provides additional context for the statements of Paul in Philippians 4:13. The Bible readily provides appropriate parameters for our actions.

Recognizing these boundaries of the larger biblical text allows us to understand exactly what meaning the author intends for us to take. If we approach Scripture in any other way, we can become manipulators of it.

Another verse to look at is this passage from the Gospel of Mark:

> And they were exceedingly astonished and said to him, "Then who can be saved?" Jesus looked at them and said, "With man it is

> impossible, but not with God. For
> all things are possible with God."
> (Mark 10:26-27)

In the context of this verse, the twelve disciples found themselves frightened at the teachings of Jesus because He explained how difficult it is for man to be saved. There was an exclusivity of salvation in Messiah's preaching, and the disciples recognized what Jesus was implying. They readily understood the severity of the situation and the disciples asked Jesus with some urgency, "Then who can be saved?"

Jesus responded that salvation through the work and hands of man is impossible—for what is required is beyond what man is capable of providing. Then the rest of the biblical record instructs us that the difficulty to purchase, acquire, and attain salvation is not ours to own. But rather, the burden of salvation is squarely placed on the outstretched shoulders and arms of Christ. It was a difficulty that He alone would have to bear—for what was impossible for man to accomplish was possible for God.

Yet, it is the phrase from this passage, "For all things are possible with God," that causes the paradox in "Can God create a rock so big He can't move it?" It is this idea of the all-encompassing, all-possible, attribute of God that makes our question so difficult to answer.

But, are we taking this comment out of context: is it true that everything is possible for God? Does Mark provide a similar situation that Paul did when Paul wrote that we can do "all" things through Christ? The latter, of course, has recognizable limits that responsible readers of the Bible would acknowledge.

So, is it possible that there are also naturally existing boundaries to God that responsible Bible readers would understand, which would provide context and parameters for the passage in Mark and other like passages?

I pose to you this question: "Can God tell a lie?"

> So when God desired to show more convincingly to the heirs of the promise the unchangeable character of his purpose, he guaranteed it with an oath, so that by two unchangeable things, in which it is impossible for God to lie, we who have fled for refuge might have strong encouragement to hold fast to the hope set before us. (Hebrews 6:17-18)

According to Hebrews, there *are* limits to what God can do. It is impossible for God to lie. He also has a character that He cannot change. He is what He is, and that is what He always will be. But besides Scripture being very clear that God cannot lie, it might be worthwhile to explain why it would not make sense for God to lie.

People tell lies because they find

themselves in some position of weakness. Even so-called "well-intentioned" lies (like lying to save someone else's life if the extreme circumstance presented itself) occur when the truth is simply too risky to tell. Lying is a result of a person realizing they are not in control, and there is a dislike of what the truth might bring. Without question, lying is a sin, because the very act and circumstances around it demonstrates something less than God.

From a spiritual perspective, we can understand why God *would never* lie, beyond the fact that the Bible says He *cannot* lie—for God is never in a position of weakness and He never fears the truth.

The passage in Hebrews also explains that God binds himself by oaths and promises, and, therefore, He further defines for us what some of His actions *must* be.

Fascinatingly enough, binding himself to certain actions is common for God. Throughout the Old Covenant, the

Scriptures record for us that God would make promises and covenants with people. He would swear oaths by the greatness of His own name. He swore by His own name, because there is no greater name that could be sworn by that could guarantee the actions that were to come.

The three-tenet promise that God made to Abraham in the beginning verses of Genesis 12, can serve as an example. God promised to Abraham that for and through his offspring He would create a great nation, provide land, and produce a blessing to all people.

This binding promise God made is called the Abrahamic Covenant. Because God cannot lie, God was incapable of breaking the covenant He made with Abraham. His covenant was going to force His hand into action at some point. (A point of interest here is that God's promise to provide land was seen in action with the rebirth of Israel as a nation in 1948. God is faithful.)

Moving on, the Bible is actually replete with boundaries and limitations on God. It is impossible for Him to lie. It is impossible for God to deny His own perfect deity by breaking some absolutes that He himself decreed. So let us look at what exactly God is limited in being.

> I am the LORD who practices steadfast love, justice, and righteousness in the earth. For in these things I delight, declares the LORD. (Jeremiah 9:24)

God's actions are in accordance with His Law. He delights in love, in being just, and in righteousness. He must reject cruelty, and is prohibited from being unjust.

> For thus says the LORD, who created the heavens (he is God!), who formed the earth and made it (he established it; he did not create it empty, he formed it to be inhabited!): "I am the LORD, and there is no other . . . I the LORD speak the truth; I declare what is right. (Isaiah 45:18-19)

God is the Creator. There is no other God. God can only declare what is right. Therefore He cannot declare, decree, or give rest, passage, or an unpaid pardon to evil, which is confirmed in Jeremiah 9:24, for He is just. He can only speak the truth.

> Before the mountains were brought forth, or ever you had formed the earth and the world, from everlasting to everlasting you are God. (Psalm 90:2)

Before the world existed, God was the existence. God is everlasting. He can never be extinguished. He is limited to a life that cannot end. He is incapable of experiencing the finality of a permanent death. And because there is no other God, and we know He is everlasting, this means there can never be another God. He is confined, throughout all of time, to be the only one of His Kind.

> You shall have no other gods before me. (Exodus 20:3)

God cannot allow humanity to persist, throughout all of time, to worship another as if they were God. This means that all, even those who deny Him now, will eventually have to worship God above all, even if that means they are bowing down from the eternal chains of hell. He cannot allow them the freedom to exist without them acknowledging His position.

> For I the LORD do not change..."
> (Malachi 3:6)

God cannot fundamentally change who and what He is. He cannot change the fact that He is everlasting. He cannot change the fact that He alone is God.

> Thus says the Lord, the King of Israel and his Redeemer, the LORD of hosts: "I am the first and I am the last; besides me there is no god.
> (Isaiah 44:6)

Multiple times the Lord decrees that He is the all-encompassing power in existence.

He is the final and only all-powerful being. He is also the rightful King of Israel. And since He is eternal, so must be His Kingship. Therefore, His kingdom of Israel must also be eternal, which also confirms His oath to Abraham.

The 32nd chapter of Deuteronomy defines for us more of what God is, and by contrast, what He can never be. We also see a term given to God that is used throughout Scripture:

> The Rock, his work is perfect, for all his ways are justice. A God of faithfulness and without iniquity, just and upright is he. (Deuteronomy 32:4)

God must operate with divine precision—He is incapable of being imperfect. God cannot be unfaithful to himself, or His promises—meaning, what He decrees, He must complete. He is upright; He cannot be corrupt.

God refers to himself as "The Rock." It is of no small importance that the theme of God labeling himself as "The Rock" begins very early in the Old Testament, for this theme is carried over into the New Testament as well.

This is a wonderful passage in the Book of Matthew where it recorded a discourse between Peter and Jesus:

> And I tell you, you are Peter, and on this rock I will build my church, and the gates of hell shall not prevail against it. (Matthew 16:18)

The English name of Peter is derived from the Greek word *Petros*. Petros means "a piece of rock." Therefore, Peter's name literally was "a piece of rock."

But in this verse, in addition to Petros, we also see the Greek word *Petra* used as well.

Jesus made a very important distinction to Peter, a distinction that our English translations fail to represent. Replacing some of the English words with the Greek, the verse would read like this, "And I tell you, you are *Petros,* and on this *Petra* I will build my church, and the gates of hell shall not prevail against it."

Undoubtedly, Jesus was pointing to himself when he said "Petra." For Petra means "a mass of rock." Petra was *not* Peter's name. Jesus literally conveyed to Peter, you are a piece of rock, and I am the mass of rock.

This is furthered confirmed in the Parable of the Tenants, which is found in Matthew, Mark, and Luke, and then is referred to again in Acts:

> This Jesus is the stone that was rejected by you, the builders, which has become the cornerstone. And there is salvation in no one else, for there is no other name under heaven given among men by which we must be saved. (Acts 4:11-12)

Jesus is the rock, the cornerstone, upon which all is built, and there cannot be another.

Shifting back to the Old Testament, in Deuteronomy, God repeatedly sets the stage and the theme for himself being named "The Rock."

> [Jeshurun] forsook God who made him and scoffed at the Rock of his salvation. (Deuteronomy 32:15)

> You were unmindful of the Rock that bore you, and you forgot the God who gave you birth. (Deuteronomy 32:18)

> For their rock is not as our Rock; our enemies are by themselves. (Deuteronomy 32:31)

In fascinating language, Deuteronomy explains that those in disobedience had false gods that they worshipped. In Deuteronomy those false gods were spoken of as "rocks," but not as "The

58

Rock." In verses 37-38, the Lord issues a direct challenge to the people about their rocks, and if those rocks are able to save them:

> Where are their gods, the rock in which they took refuge . . . Let them rise up and help you; let them be your protection! (Deuteronomy 32:37-38)

Understanding the fuller breadth of Scripture, we know God refers to himself as "The Rock," and false gods were smaller rocks. Why was that?

It is because the worshippers of Baal and other false idols would use real rocks in the worship of their false gods. They would set up, in their pagan temples and altars, large stones, and claim those stones represented their gods. They literally worshipped rocks.

Keeping with God's character to use language His people could understand, God relayed to His prophets that He was "The Rock," which meant to those people of that era, that He was The God, and there were no other gods, or other rocks. This brings clarity to Deuteronomy 32:37-38 when the Lord challenges people to see if their rocks can rescue them. He then continues to say in verse 39: "See now that I, even I, am he, and there is no god beside me; . . ."

After the failure of people to be delivered by their god, their rock, the Lord said, see now that I am "The Rock" the *Only God.*

That brings us to the shocking and vast implication behind our age old Rock Paradox, "Can God create a rock so big He can't move it?"

The question is a far more brazen assertion than simply asking if there is a mass of hardened mud and sand that God could make that got too big for Him to shovel away. The question is an outright challenge to the Lordship and deity of God, regardless if the modern church even understands this.

"Can God create a rock so big He can't move it?" is literally asking, "Can the created ever become greater than the Creator?" Can the Petros be greater than the Petra? Can God ever become the lesser of two wills? Can the demonic idol ever rise above the one and only true God?

When all the data is known, suddenly what seemed to be an unsolvable paradox is now stunningly simple. Even more so, the question is not silly at all. In fact, the question is at the heart of the original sin of Adam and in the heart of our adversary, Satan. Yet it is posed in such a subtle and deceptive way.

I believe the Rock Paradox was a question seeded by Satan out of arrogant defiance. It was also meant to mock the spiritual and biblical ignorance of the broader western church—for Satan knew using "rock" as the object would only magnify the embarrassment of our failure. This question has demonstrated that even many of our seminary leaders are so underequipped theologically that they could not even answer a question about God's ultimate claim to exclusive divinity.

So, "Can God create a rock so big He can't move it?" Can there ever be another rock that can stand triumphantly against the will of God?

The apostasy of the question was hidden in plain sight. The absolute answer is "No!"

God cannot create a rock, an idol, a being, a god, an angel, a country, a nation, a universe, a man, that is too big for Him to move, control, define, and judge. God's limitation is in himself. He is the only God. There is none greater, there never can be. All of existence from everlasting to everlasting is confined to be under the greatness of God. And this confinement extends to God. He is confined to be the greatest, and He is incapable of creating anything greater than himself.

Is there a God besides me? There is no Rock; I know not any." (Isaiah 44:8)

# CHAPTER FIVE

# SOFT TARGET

◆ ◆ ◆

The crescendo of final thoughts in the previous chapter certainly did feel like the climax. But we still have a fair distance to run. The purpose I have undertaken is not to just offer a solution to the Rock Paradox question, for if that was my simple goal, then we could be simply done.

The larger task is to tackle a far more ominous and complex question: Why is it Christians struggled with this question to begin with? One would think that the verdict of "No" should have been a quick reflex we all offered.

I fear our discernment has been compromised and the emergency flares have long been shot and completely ignored. Indeed, our lack of spiritual direction in America can be seen in every one of our 360 degrees. We are murdering untold numbers through abortion and our televisions are replete with sexual material. Our fall has been so great that terms like open marriage are replacing adultery, abortion has replaced murder, and alternative lifestyle has replaced the sin of sodomy.

With such tidal turns in our society, are we even justified in being surprised that evil seems to be winning in our streets and our youth are succumbing to debauchery at alarming rates? The Bible belt of the U.S. has become unbuckled and many of those who should respond are focused elsewhere.

Too many churches have become businesses with CEO's instead of pastors, club members instead of elders, and entertainers instead of worshippers. It is as if the church has outsourced its management to the world.

And in becoming so much like the world, we, the born again, have abandoned our position of authority. This abdication has allowed secularists, avowed atheists, and other religions to redefine our government, our neighborhoods, and our schools. We have allowed the secular world to determine the boundaries of appropriate behavior and even the church has become a willing canvas as the world has repainted us in their image.

Not the least of these paint jobs is the revision of humanities origin. The modern church has allowed the powers of secular academia to condemn the foundation of our beliefs and rip us from our Jewish origins of the Old Covenant. A reoccurring theme in this book is the point that the modern church has abandoned the divinely inspired Jewish history of the Old Testament. Yet, Christianity is the name given to the belief that Jesus, or Yeshua, was the foretold Jewish Messiah and, therefore, He is the completion to the Judaism of the Old Covenant. But when the modern church rejects the history of our Jewish foundation, then they are rejecting what Jesus came to complete. So where does that leave Christianity? It leaves it standing on a false foundation that is now easily moved.

Nowhere is this seen more poignantly than the attack on Genesis and the six-day creation. One of the titans of atheistic thought is the scientist Stephen Hawking. Hawking has unapologetically pushed the wildly subjective Big Bang theory as the story of our origins, as opposed to the account given to us in our Bible. Recognize that whenever humanities origins are challenged, that it is a direct assault on the Bible—for the Bible has already given us the answer to our origins.

In an article that carries a Babel-like arrogance entitled, "Why God Did Not Create the Universe," look at what Hawking and Leonard Mlodinow invoked to replace God as a creator:

> As recent advances in cosmology suggest, the laws of gravity and quantum theory allow universes to appear spontaneously from nothing. Spontaneous creation is the reason there is something rather than nothing, why the universe exists, why we exist.[3]

The evolutionary-driven atheists, the haters of the Bible, have fallen in their folly to such depths that they have replaced God with the illogical conclusion that out of nothing sprang everything.

---

3    Stephen Hawking and Leonard Mlodinow, *Why God Did Not Create the Universe*, Wall Street Journal, Retrieved on September 9, 2010

These men are not alone. The cover of a prominent scientific journal offered a summation of an article contained within by cosmologist Alan Guth, proponent of the inflation model of the Big Bang. It stated:

> The universe burst into something from absolutely nothing—zero, nada. And as it got bigger, it became filled with even more stuff that came from absolutely nowhere.[4]

The conclusion that everything came from nothing is patent absurdity. Yet, what have most seminaries and many churches done in response to this Big Bang idea? They have accepted it and apologize for the creation account found in the Bible! They have rejected the history that Jesus came to complete.

Let's not forget that the Big Bang theory of origins promotes the idea that billions

---

4    "Guth's Grand Guess," Discover, vol. 23, p. 35, April 2002.

of stars and planets were all formed out of something so small that *it* nearly had the value of zero, and that it came from nothing. I have seen the Big Bang explained in that this infinitesimal point of beginnings, which all the universe sprang from, was no bigger than the size of a pinhead.

To try to rationalize the absurdity of the anti-Bible/Big Bang position, read what astrophysicist, Dr. Jason Lisle, says on the massive amount of energy output that just our sun and galaxy produces, let alone the entire universe.

> The sun alone gives off more energy every second than one billion major cities would produce in one year. Yet, our entire galaxy is 20 billion times more luminous than the sun.[5]

Yet, secular scientists would like us to believe that all of that massive power

5    Dr. Jason Lisle, *Taking Back Astronomy*, Master Books, 2009, pg. 21

was contained in a tiny little point the size of a pinhead, which created itself out of nothing! The Big Bang, like the rock paradox, is another example that our ability to think has been disabled. Something has broken inside of us and our spiritual discernment has decayed, and our wisdom has receded. This has happened, because we no longer turn to the Bible for instruction, and when we do, we have learned to make our beliefs shape what was written instead of allowing the Bible to shape us.

The truth of the matter is this, our origin and purpose were never supposed to be a puzzle. God did not create the world so that the enigma of our existence would confound us. This is confirmed in the Book of Romans:

> For what can be known about God is plain to them, because God has shown it to them. For his invisible attributes, namely, his eternal power

and divine nature, have been clearly perceived, ever since the creation of the world, in the things that have been made. So they are without excuse. (Romans 1:19-20)

The Lord provided His Son, Jesus the Messiah. The Lord gave us the Scriptures, the functions of reason, the design in nature, and the need for fellowship. He made an entire chosen people, through whom He brought to the world the moral law. Later, through the apostles, they would be the first missionary force to the world to speak boldly about His plan and grace, and the world has never been the same since. He has done all of this to provide evidence of His existence and to leave all without excuse.

But the Bible specifically warns us that we can be deceived from seeing the evidence if we are not disciplined in our spiritual walk. We can be deceived if our minds are not protected from the enemy.

> See to it that no one takes you captive
> by philosophy and empty deceit,
> according to human tradition,
> according to the elemental spirits
> of the world, and not according to
> Christ. (Colossians 2:8)

We must have the wisdom to understand that there are philosophies that are designed to take us prisoner. And when our mind is captured by empty deceit, that deceit keeps the evidence from being seen, which can leave us quite vulnerable to believing lies.

This is why the Bible uses such imagery as applying armor to our mind and spirit.

> Therefore take up the whole armor
> of God, that you may be able
> to withstand in the evil day, and
> having done all, to stand firm. Stand
> therefore, having fastened on the
> belt of truth, and having put on the
> breastplate of righteousness, and, as
> shoes for your feet, having put on

the readiness given by the gospel of peace. In all circumstances take up the shield of faith, with which you can extinguish all the flaming darts of the evil one; and take the helmet of salvation, and the sword of the Spirit, which is the word of God, praying at all times in the Spirit, with all prayer and supplication. (Ephesians 6:13-18)

Most of us do not live in this full armor of God. We walk the streets and ingest media of all kinds without pause or caution. This reckless habit exposes the soft target of our mind, and our adversary has hunted and harvested well.

But hope is not gone. We serve a powerful God, and He is able to right our path. But we must earnestly seek after Him and commit ourselves to wisdom, understanding, and knowledge.

In this journey to equip our minds, I believe a quick overview of the secular philosophies modernism and postmodernism can help us identify the assaults coming against our mind. The hope is that once we understand the assault we will be able to stand against this moral entropy that we see all around us.

# CHAPTER SIX

# SECULAR SOIL

◆ ◆ ◆

The most defining characteristic of modernism and postmodernism is that both are worldviews, which are grown from secular soils. The philosophies, in their base make-up, reject the authority and reality of God.

Dealing with modernism first, it generally refers to the set of secular ideals that developed in the era that followed the Renaissance and the Reformation. The five points that I have condensed below were certainly not all immediately adopted in a definitive manifesto at the end of a specific period, but rather modernism grew to be a clotting of ideas that collected over time.

## Modernism[6] [7]

1. *Naturalism/Materialism:* In our present day, naturalism is used interchangeably with the term materialism. Materialism is the belief that natural (material) laws can exhaustively explain all of nature. Therefore, our permissible knowledge bank is confined to what can be observed or proven by man.

Essentially, if mankind cannot see it, or definitively prove it, then it cannot exist. Materialism is the prominent philosophy held by secular scientists today. It rejects any intervention by the divine.

This rejection of a supreme creator naturally creates an overarching assumption that material, in essence, simply created itself.

---

6    *The Popular Encyclopedia of Apologetics,* Harvest House, 2008, Pg.349
7    *The Popular Encyclopedia of Apologetics,* Harvest House, 2008, pg. 398

And with that, I believe a key concept is grasped. Modernism is built on the idea that everything that we see around us, from matter, molecules, to man was ultimately self-created.

When the secular world points to Christianity and claims our faith is not based on rationale or reason, the Christian needs only to remember these claims of materialism.

2. *Humanism: Humanism* is the natural extension of materialism, which rejects any idea of God. Humanism comes complete with its own doctrine. The first two tenets of the Humanist Manifesto of 1933 state this:

1. Religious humanists regard the universe as self-existing and not created.

2. Humanism believes that man is a part of nature and has emerged as a result of continuous process.

Note the *religion* of humanism states man is self-created through nature. It also assumes man is the pinnacle of existence because we appear to be the most evolved creature, at least on this planet. Humanism not only removes God, it makes man god, or as Stephen Hawking puts it:

> Although we are puny and insignificant on the scale of the cosmos, this makes us in a sense the lords of creation.[8]

Humanism is the maturation of the original sin of Adam and the lie of the serpent in Genesis 3. From the beginning man has had a desire to be his own lord of creation. Humanism is the pandemic viral outbreak of the original sin of Adam. Yet, oddly enough, when humanism removes God and, therefore, His divine purpose for us, man becomes puny and insignificant. Yet, the humanists still tout us as lords of creation, even though their worldview has

---

8    Stephen Hawking and Leonard Mlodinow, "Why God Did Not Create the Universe," WSJ.com, September 9, 2010

made us puny and insignificant. Here we witness the confusion of the scoffer.

In a lesson that cannot be forgotten, whenever we devaluate God we devaluate ourselves. This outcome is a product of divine design. God put His fingerprint on us, so that when we remove Him, we lose any worthwhile identity in ourselves. This is, quite possibly, the most brilliant design feature I have yet to see.

3. *Science:* The first two tenets of materialism and humanism essentially proclaim man as the measure. Therefore, we can recognize how science became the governing authority for the philosophy of modernism—for it is how man gathers data and then makes conclusions. Thus scientists in lab coats replaced the priests in robes as the purveyors of knowledge. And the idea that "you can't fight science" has rolled forward ever since.

The next two concepts of modernism are closely related and I am weaving them into one for our use.

4. *Reductionism and Nature:* These ideas essentially state that mankind is only a highly advanced animal and product of naturalistic evolution. We are simply reduced to creatures, driven by instinct. In 1859, Charles Darwin widely popularized the theory of evolution when he published *On the Origin of Species by Means of Natural Selection, or the Preservation of Favoured Races in the Struggle for Life.* This book was instrumental in cementing this secular worldview and it became an inseparable key to modernism.

The next requirement for modernism is something that has, interestingly enough, become a buzzword for today—Progress.

5. *Progress:* Woven deeply into modernism is the idea that man is always progressing. It is from this ideology that the term "progressives" most certainly comes. The line of thinking, that is progressivism, is

not complicated to follow if one holds fast to the previous tenets of modernism.

This view argues that if all of nature is self-made, and through the passing of time everything evolves and continues to advance into greater complexity. Therefore, all of nature would always be getting better with time.

This kind of rationale breeds the idea that whatever is next is best. This also would deem anything that stands in the way of *progress* as undesirable.

Works of old, whether it is the Bible, or the even the U.S. Constitution, can be quickly accused of being outdated. Progress could demand that we improve, update, or disregard the ancient relics and move forward. This kind of mentality causes difficulties in establishing an authority, because at any point, in the name of progress, the older ideas, laws, and beliefs can be readily dispatched.

A cursory look at our culture today, especially in the western world, reveals cultures that have been heavily influenced by modernism.

But in the 21st century, on the heels of modernism came another secular worldview, which is *postmodernism.*

## Postmodernism

This is essentially the search for individual significance without any external controls. It is the idea that everything is relative to the individual. In this philosophy, the truth is only that in which you decide for yourself. This gives rise to the statement that we often hear, "What is true for you, is not necessarily true for me."

Postmodern philosophers like Derrida, Lyotard, and Foucalt perpetuated the idea that there is no universal truth.[9] But the critic of postmodernism would quickly ask, "Is it true that there is no truth?"

---

9    *The Popular Encyclopedia of Apologetics,* Harvest House Publishers, 2008, pg. 400

It is here we see the breakdown of postmodernism. The base premise of postmodernism, which states there is no absolute truth, is actually an assertion of an absolute truth. Postmodernism, in its most simplistic form, is very easy to understand, though it itself is not understandable. Understand?

The postmodern conflict with the Bible is apparent. The Bible claims an exclusive and non-bending absolute truth about the deity of Jesus the Messiah.

> Jesus said to him, "I am the way, and the truth, and the life. No one comes to the Father except through me." (John 14:6)

John recorded for us an unwavering assertion of absolute truth from Jesus himself. However, the principles in postmodernism allow the readers, not the author, to determine the truth of a written text for themselves.

Therefore, the original intent of the author is discarded and replaced by the interpretational motives of the postmodern individual. This means that the written word, in any form, becomes bastardized with no father of origin. *So in postmodernism even the inspired Scriptures become whatever the reader deems them to mean.*

As an example, a postmodern thinker would look at John 14:6 and might say:

"What does it mean to me that Jesus was claiming that he was the only way, the truth and the life? This was certainly true for Jesus—for I have no right to tell him that he was wrong for himself. To me though, it appears that Jesus was the first postmodern because he recognized his truth, his way, and his life was found solely inside of himself. Jesus recognized that he decided what truth was. Just like Jesus, my journey goes through my way, my truth, and my life. Jesus was teaching that we all can find our own way to truth through ourselves."

Using the deception of postmodernism, one can see the perversion that can ensue. The Bible teaches an absolute exclusivity of Jesus being the only way to salvation. Yet, through the doors of postmodernism, where truth is relative to the individual, the clearest statements can become an endorsement for anything the individual wishes them to be.

The postmodern environment does not produce anything that would lead someone to believe that they have sinned against an Almighty God. There is nothing within this philosophy that would hint to the individual that they have been wrong, and that they need to repent to and obey a higher authority. In fact, postmodernism seems to be a perfect doctrine for damnation.

These secular philosophies have been tactics used to make humanity a vulnerable prey. But notice how the effect of these philosophies has been cumulative. We cannot point to just one of these ideologies and say, this is where the westernized world is at—for the moods and beliefs of the secular world are always in flux, and, quite frankly, it is going from bad to worse.

In our present day, most of the secular West has adopted an amalgamation of modernism and postmodernism into one messy philosophy of life. I have termed it *Postmodern Progressivism*. It is defined with five major points:

1. *Humanism:* Man is the pinnacle of all things

2. *Materialism:* What can be seen and tested is all that there is.

3. *Relativism:* There is no absolute truth; all is relative to the individual

4. *Evolution:* All of nature is a product of random chance, through the Big Bang and has evolved through Darwinian measures.

5. *Progressivism:* Liberal government can create and manage a sustainable utopia advancing humanity and the planet.

The observer will notice these points have obvious friction and contradiction with each other. Point and case, the Big Bang, or anything like it has never been observed, tested, or proven, and the same goes with evolution. But secular science still believes in both, at the exact same time they tout materialism as being absolute. Nevertheless, this is the incongruent belief system of so many in westernized society. Yet too many Christians, instead of being the urgent voice of reason, have fallen mute and given way to the many deceptions.

We need to condition our minds to be able to identify in our culture and in our homes where Postmodern Progressivism has taken root. Because if we want a strong spiritual life that will pay dividends in this life and the next, we need to eradicate this cancer of secular philosophy from every aspect of our lives.

# CHAPTER SEVEN

# OPPRESSION

◆ ◆ ◆

Be aware, and take note of the move of the adversary. Train your eyes to catch this. He has kept on with his original deception. He began with Adam and Eve, convincing them that they could be as God. Now, approximately 6,000 years later, he is still selling the same line. He is convincing people that we all should establish our own truth and be our own lords over creation. His entire attack on humanity has never changed. It is centered on us being our own gods. If you can identify this, you can stop it in your life and your families.

Notice the packaging into which he has put this original sin today. He has made the stupid, simple sin of man's pride into something academic, sophisticated, and progressive. It is now oh so progressive to determine your own truth. It is a status symbol to disregard the ancient and laughable words of God. And people are buying this hook, line, and sinker.

Once this oppression of the mind is accomplished in an individual, they begin viewing the world through their own lens, no matter what shade it might be. This creates an environment that even when God is speaking, man consciously decides to change God's meaning for his meaning, God's control for his control, God's words into his words. Everything becomes a web of confusion.

Obviously, buying into what the adversary is selling is not a wise practice. When someone anoints themselves as their only rightful judge, then virtues and values like discipline, constructive criticism, and even authority figures are driven out from their self-glorifying temples. The "council of many" is the anathema of postmodern progressives where no council is greater than their own.

If an entire society starts to be built on postmodern progressivism, there will be an epic collapse of that society. The empire of man will be choked out under the heel of his own boot. Proverbs tells us:

> Where there is no guidance, a people falls, but in an abundance of counselors there is safety. (Proverbs 11:14)

The fact is, true growth comes from first realizing that help cannot come from ourselves, but that we need the great Helper to intercede and to fix our course. Self-help living does not work. We need help. We need His help.

> But the Helper, the Holy Spirit, whom the Father will send in my name, he will teach you all things and bring to your remembrance all that I have said to you. (John 14:26)

But we have been blinded from this truth, and our adversary has helped many to think we have control. Every secular force has been engineered to make us believe that within the human comes the power and the facilities to determine our own truth and reality. But is this true?

Each of our lives has bookends we do not control. We were born without our choice, permission, or consent. We will die without ultimate counsel ever being sought. Our certain death will happen on a day that we will never know until that singular final moment when it becomes clear our earthly journey has finally run out.

Recognizing this fact is only the beginning of realizing our severe limitations. We were each given a set of genetic capabilities that we did not choose or assemble; our parents and siblings where provided for us without our input; our bodies, genders, tastes, and talents we did not choose.

I, for one, like the taste of honey; my brother does not. Neither of us was given a checklist before life where I said I would choose honey as a flavor of choice, whereas he did not. Every action that we make is preceded by an inclination of our nature, and our nature is a product of our genes, and our genes stretch back to the product and vision of our Creator. They did not come of our own volition.

Do you ever ask yourself how much air each day you will need to breathe? Or is it just there waiting for you? Do you ever ask yourself to schedule your heartbeats for the day, or plan out how many blinks your eyes will need to take, or how to prepare for the number of thoughts you will have? Or doesn't it all just happen for you as a machine that was neither built by you nor seeks your instruction on how to run?

We think thoughts with a brain that was not our creation, which is stimulated by everything around us, which was not our creation. We breathe in oxygen, just always believing the next breath will be there, even though we have no power if it is or if it is not.

Your eyes were opened at your birth and you began to see without any will or decision from yourself. Your body tells you when it is hungry, tells you when you are tired, forces you to sleep, and wakes you when you are done. If you try to fight your body, it is a short fight, and your body always wins. How much control do you really think you have?

Philosophically, many of us have decided that we control our destiny, and we are a product of our own making. Yet in reality, we take out policies of health insurance, homeowners insurance, life insurance, automobile insurance, flood insurance, business insurance, crop insurance, livestock insurance, pet insurance, vacation insurance, etc., etc., etcetera.

We always are trying to insure against the unexpected, because we are learning that our expectations are rarely ever met. Even though we give lip service to the ideas of control, our lives say something else.

Then we must consider the wonder of what we see in the mirror. Medicinal sciences are simply trying to understand, through trial and error, the amazing mechanism of our body, which is exponentially more advanced than our understanding of it.

We are trying to learn why certain things happen, why certain things don't, and, of course, how to prolong life. It is the latter in which we have always hit a dead end.

Man loves to tout the achievement of his technology and parade the advancements of what he can create. Each of us stands in wonder at the amazing computer advancements and the ability to store vast amount of data on tiny little chips. Yet did you know our own body dwarfs all of our advancements by orders of magnitude?

As an example, the information stored in a dot of DNA is 100 million times more than what can be stored in a 40-gigabyte hard drive. Next, try to fathom how much DNA we actually have. If we took the DNA in the human body and joined it like a rope, end to end, it would wrap around the Earth's equator three and a half million times![10]

The data needed to run each one of our bodies is an astronomical figure. And the advanced design to store such data, and then to access it seamlessly and automatically in all of our day-to-day functions is a technology that humanity

10   Creation Ex Nihilo 17 (4): 10-13

simply can't fathom. It should be humbling to recognize that as much as mankind does know, we do not even know enough to fully understand ourselves.

Yet here we are. We have somehow convinced ourselves that our own knowledge, and our own science, is the measure in which everything must be weighed. We do this even though every day we look in the mirror and see a body whose miraculous design far outpaces, by exponential degrees, any advancement man has attained.

In light of this, we have people who are so arrogant and so convoluted, confused, and dismayed that they think they are the "lords of creation." Such a conclusion should not be allowed in the door of a rational conversation. But as we should know by now, those who reject God, already reject the rational. So we should not be surprised.

It is on this precipice that we now stand. Our wisdom is not maturing at the same rate our bodies are aging. Our discernment is buried under layers of secular philosophical debris. This attack has wounded the Bible believers who are called to be the missionary force to the world to spread the light of our divine Father. Without a doubt, if the adoption of sons and daughters into the Kingdom of Messiah was dependent on our disciplined approach to spiritual maturity, then we would have certainly left the world an orphanage. Thank the Lord for grace and mercy.

# CHAPTER EIGHT

# MINDLESS

◆ ◆ ◆

I attended an event in St. Louis where my publisher, Bridge Logos, arranged a book-signing event for my second release, *Dragons or Dinosaurs.* One of the people standing in line was a nice man and a self-proclaiming Christian. When it was his turn, he said to me, essentially, "No one really knows for sure what is true, we simply have to believe."

I think he was referring to a six-day creation in the book of Genesis, but he did not specifically isolate his comment to such. He looked at me inquisitively, seemingly waiting for me to confirm his statement and, thereby, oddly comfort each other that we are fellow travelers on this road of hope, which apparently has no evidence of such hope.

To be completely honest, I think I did a fairly good job of masking my astonishment at his statement. Instead of delivering a monologue, I told him in short fashion, (for there was a long line of people waiting behind him) that from what I have examined, all the evidence of the world points to not merely an intelligent designer but to Christ the Creator.

This common proposition that Bible believers accept a blind faith is a soapbox issue for me, from which I don't think I will ever step down. I asked the gentleman to read the book he had just received with an eager mind to learn.[11] If he would, evidence is presented there that confirms

---

11    Darek Isaacs, *Dragons or Dinosaurs,* Bridge-Logos, 2010

the Bible and that would help him find more certainty in the hope he holds.

Much like that gentleman, many Christians are often quite soft on their declarations of faith, despite the overwhelming evidence. This softness is not out of necessity—it is out of ignorance. The foundation that our Scriptures stand on is of the highest grade. The problem is people have not equipped their mind for the race at hand. We have been lulled into a fog of an odd surrealism.

The piercing truth is, the risen Christ left us ample evidence to confidently express His divine Kingship. The shadow of ambiguity is not a place where the Lord resides. He is the light so that all can see. He breaks through the darkness if people will just open their eyes and seek.

In addition to the naturalistic evidence that shines on the handiwork of a Creator, there is also the gift of reason with which humanity has been endowed. It is my firm conviction our Lord created the functions of reason to make a step of faith the rational step to make.

We have been given the mind to see the stairway of repentance and grace that connects our front porch to His throne. So those who refuse to take the first step of humility are without excuse. Those who do not see Him are those who willfully look away. Those who reject Him do so, not out of the lack of evidence of Him, but because of a natural depravity that pushes them to reject the authority of God.

This is confirmed in the Bible, the merciful revelation of evidence, second only to the incarnation of Christ.

> For what can be known about God is plain to them, because God has shown it to them. For *his invisible attributes, namely, his eternal power and divine nature, have been clearly perceived,* ever since the creation of the world, in the things that have been made.

*So they are without excuse.* (Romans 1:19-20, italics mine)

Willfully looking away can take many forms, and do not think looking away applies only to the apostates, atheists, and pagans. If the Bible believer does not see God clearly, then that is the failure of the individual—for we are told that if we seek, we will find. This is a promise from our Lord.

We must understand that not having the heart to earnestly seek Him is the same thing as willfully looking away. Lack of discipline, so that we have not equipped our mind to understand what deceptions have taken a hold of us, is a manner of looking away. Living a lukewarm spiritual life that is uneducated on spiritual matters is the same thing as willfully strapping on blinders. For what can be known of God has been shown to us and is clearly perceivable, if we only have the simple desire to seek. We all stand without excuse for not having a deeper relationship with our Lord.

I see nothing that leads me to believe that blind faith is our call; that wishful thinking is our foundation. God created mankind to be able to readily perceive, recognize, and deduce His divine presence. But we do not all see, do we?

Life looks hazy, uncertain, and unsteady. Can we not see that His hands are open, that the victory is His—that the answers to our existence are readily available? Christ is shining on. He is like a City on the Hill. He is offering illumination, while we are choosing to walk in darkness and too many think our blessed hope is only slightly better than a false hope.

However, Romans 1:19 explains that His glory, presence, and deity is here for all to see.

Therefore, if everything is so clear, why have so many fallen to uncertainty? The book of Colossians speaks to this.

See to it that no one takes you captive by philosophy and empty deceit, according to human tradition, according to the elemental spirits of the world, and not according to Christ. (Colossians 2:8)

The enemy, Satan, has taken us captive with hollow and false philosophy. He has employed a systematic attack through modernism and postmodernism to cripple our rationale, and beat our minds with the dullest side of a club. Mankind has succumbed and has imbibed a steady stream of deceptive secular thought that has taken its toll on our ability to discern and make sense of the world around us.

The reason this attack has found its victims is because we do not love the Lord our God with our entire *mind*.

"You shall love the Lord your God with all your heart and with all your soul and with all your strength and *with all your mind,* and your neighbor as yourself." (Luke 10:27, italics mine)

The commandment that is often overlooked in this verse is the commandment that this book is focused on. We are to love with our mind. Our minds were given to us as an asset. These mental capacities of ours were designed to one end alone: so that we can recognize our indebtedness to the Creator and then enter into a repentance and fellowship with Him (and in that order). It is for this reason the deceiver of the whole world has labored to beat us mindless.

We have reached a point, and we see it on the news constantly, that our decisions make less and less sense every day. Up is down, black is white, and no clear answer can ever be found. Politicians that we elect actually make it a career to cause confusion. That is the key to their election, and we have put them in power over us.

We need to find a radical heart for change. Mankind has become consumed with foolishness, immaturity, and a lack of discipline. This has imprisoned our thinking and arrested our judgment. It is exactly where the adversary wants us to be. It is time to put away the foolish things of this world, and renew fervor for the Lord. This comes from studying His Word, obeying His will, and worshipping at His feet. These are daily tasks.

# CHAPTER NINE

# THE LIGHT OF REASON

◆ ◆ ◆

As we set out to create a disciplined approach to being disciples of our Lord, I believe it will be valuable to give a short and simple introduction to logical reasoning. Having a working understanding of the information in this chapter will pay deep dividends in the subsequent chapters.

The Lord properly equipped us with miraculous minds and the ability to reason so that we would rightly conclude that God is, and was, and ever will be. Reason is the friend of the Bible believer.

This brings us to the important distinctions between terms that most are familiar with: deductive reasoning and inductive reasoning.

*Deductive reasoning* is an argument that moves from a general statement to a particular one. It moves from a broad assessment to a narrow conclusion. As an example:

> If all men need to breathe oxygen, and I am a man, then I need to breathe oxygen.

This is a deductive argument, and it is logically valid. The broad assessment was that all men need to breathe oxygen. The narrow conclusion was that if I am a man I must breathe oxygen.

But does deductive reasoning always lead to the truth? No, it does not. The key to deductive reasoning hinges on the premises being true. Here is an example of what I mean:

All birds have feathers.

Humans are birds.

Therefore, all humans have feathers.

Believe it or not, this is actually a valid argument! It is logically deduced. However, something is obviously wrong. The problem in this statement is that one or more of the premises in the conditional proposition is not truthful. In this case, humans are not birds.

Deductive reasoning does not judge the truth of the premises; it simply creates a model so that a decision can be reached if the premises *are* true. Therefore, there can be a difference between a valid argument, and a truthful argument.

So even though an argument is valid, the true or sound conclusion is dependent on the truth of the premises.

*Inductive reasoning,* however, works in a different "direction" than deductive reasoning. Whereas, deductive begins with a general premise and then moves to a particular conclusion, inductive reasoning begins with a particular sampling and then makes a broad, general, conclusion. Here is an example:

Water quenches my thirst.

Water is a liquid.

Therefore, all liquids would quench my thirst.

This is an example of inductive reasoning. It moves from a particular item with a particular occurrence and then produces a broad conclusion. It is very easy to see how this kind of reasoning leads to logical failures. For even though water is a liquid that does quench my thirst, certainly there are many types of liquids that would not quench my thirst and many would make me more thirsty.

Clearly, inductive reasoning as a model to make decisions is logically fallacious. If someone rushes to conclusions and is hasty or biased in reaching an outcome, inductive reasoning can lead to very wrong conclusions.

Inductive reasoning, however, does not always lead to failure. As an example:

> The water in my cup is pure.
>
> The water in my cup is safe for me to drink.
>
> Therefore, all pure water on earth is safe for me to drink.

A small sample of purified water was used to make a generalized conclusion about all purified water. In this particular case, the answer is true. This is inductive reasoning. It takes a small sampling of data, and then produces a conclusion, which is applied to the entire field. The danger of inductive reasoning is the exhaustive field of data is usually unattainable and, therefore, the conclusion cannot be absolutely verified.

One of the limitations of mankind is that we are finite. This creates the situation where inductive reasoning is our only option much of the time. So, even though it is not ideal, we are only human and our naturally existing limitations corner us into using inductive reasoning every day.

One example of inductive reasoning is observed heading into a political election. The political polls are an attempt to gauge the sentiments of the broader population by only sampling a few. The sample often consists of about 1,000 likely voters, which are the sample group. Pollsters provide a survey to the sample group and then the results are extrapolated to make a judgment on the entire population. This is inductive reasoning in practice.

In the presidential election of 2004, some exit polling at the voting centers suggested that John Kerry was going to win the presidential election. Some of the media outlets actually started to call the election in certain areas. However, when the entire breadth of data was mined and examined, it proved the conclusions of some of the exit polls to be in error. George W. Bush won the election. Thus, we see an example of the natural shortcomings of the professional application of inductive reasoning.

Mankind must use inductive reasoning for much of what we do, but we can never forget the inherent limitations and sometimes flawed decisions that can arise due to its nature.

The Lord gave us the ability to use reason and the sensibility to discern the difference between deductive reasoning and inductive reasoning, so that when we see a powerful truth that has no bend, we can recognize it. This mercy was not given in haste. It was not a flippant decision of our Creator to endow us with this kind of reasoning and understanding.

# CHAPTER TEN

# THE EXCELLENCE

◆ ◆ ◆

It is my assumption that most of us have not realized the true excellence of the biblical faith as a reasoned worldview. It is an excellence designed to evict doubt from our minds and to dislodge any barnacles of indecision about the solid rock on which we stand.

God gave us simplicity in the faith of Jesus, who was the Messiah foretold in the Old Testament, and then revealed in the New Testament. This faith is a faith of deductive reasoning. It is a logically valid faith. It begins with an authoritative broad truth, which is the widely encompassing Word of God. Then, we deduce, starting from this truth, the workings of the world and the meaning of life.

With divine precision, the Lord provided one premise upon which faith rises or falls. If this one premise is true, then there is a landslide of consequences and conclusions that can be logically deduced to be valid and sound. If this one premise is false, then the Bible and all of its tenets and beliefs are unsound conclusions. The latter would mean the belief in Jesus as the foretold Messiah, Lord and Creator, would fail. I will not mince words on this. It is an all or nothing deal.

The one event that ultimately matters is the resurrection of Jesus the Messiah. The resurrection is the all-powerful premise that, if true, leads to the sound deduction that all of the history of the Bible is, in fact, the authoritative Word of God. Therefore, it could be supremely trusted and all the doctrines of the biblical faith would hold true. This includes the 6-day creation, the global Flood, the Tower of Babel, the Salvation of Man, and the eternal destinations of every human soul in either the Kingdom of God, with their Lord and Messiah, or in hell, forever separated from God's glory.

Indeed, the weight of the implication is so heavy that we must all answer this question: *Did Jesus rise from the dead?*— for the answer to this question determines absolutely everything.

Please understand, this book is not attempting an exhaustive apologetic for the resurrection of Messiah. Volumes of work have already been devoted to this. I am aiming to demonstrate conclusions on the matter and using them to illustrate the deductive nature of Christianity.

When considering this question, understand there is true historicity about the claims of the resurrection.

The resurrection is not about a blind belief if we are to place any value on written and oral history. We have history that Jesus was killed through the crucifixion, and then we have eyewitnesses of Jesus walking around *after* He was known to be dead and buried.

Lee Strobel argues that the evidence for the resurrection is overwhelming.

> "Without question, the amount of testimony and corroboration of Jesus' post-Resurrection appearances is staggering. To put it into perspective, if you were to call each one of the witnesses to a court of law to be cross-examined for just fifteen minutes each, and you went around the clock without a break, it would take you from breakfast on Monday until dinner on Friday to hear them all. After listening to 129 straight hours of eyewitness

testimony, who could possibly walk away unconvinced?"[12]

Furthermore, if anyone had produced the dead body of Jesus after the claims of the resurrection, Christianity would have been terminated on the spot. But that never happened.

We must all take into account that Jesus, the most well-known Jewish man in the region, was publicly crucified in front of the masses. Then the authorities applied powerful measures to prevent a resurrection hoax, because they were aware that Jesus had claimed He would rise from the dead.

Next day, that is, after the day of Preparation, the chief priests and the Pharisees gathered before Pilate and said, "Sir, we remember how that impostor said, while he was still alive, 'After three days I will rise.' Therefore order the tomb to be

12    Lee Strobel, *A Case for Christ*, Zondervan, pg. 237

> made secure until the third day, lest his disciples go and steal him away and tell the people, 'He has risen from the dead,' and the last fraud will be worse than the first." Pilate said to them, "You have a guard of soldiers. Go, make it as secure as you can." So they went and made the tomb secure by sealing the stone and setting a guard. (Matthew 27:62-66)

Yet, even with Roman security, the claims to the resurrection still happened, and no one ever produced the dead body or witnesses to prove otherwise.

Furthermore, those claiming to have seen the resurrected Messiah with their own eyes were unwilling to deny it even under the threat of death—and those threats were not empty. It did end up costing the lives of many of those who made the unwavering claim.

It bears mentioning that people will die for something that they think is true, but they will not die for something that they know is a lie. The apostles and many others claimed eyewitness accounts of seeing and talking with Jesus after His resurrection. If the resurrection was a lie, then it was their lie, and they knew it.

People who die for their religion today are much different in their makeup. They were not eyewitnesses to what happened, they are moving on faith. If their religion is a lie, then they were fooled, because they think it is true. However, the first church was not like this. Every single one of the apostles, excluding John, were executed because they would not deny what they saw with their own eyes. This is not the sign of people perpetrating a hoax.

Therefore, if you and I become convicted of the truth of the resurrection, then this leads to the understanding that death, something that all of mankind faces, could not hold Jesus the Messiah. He did not stay dead!

His resurrection testified to the fact that He was not merely a man. For no man in history has been able to resurrect himself from the dead. Especially after being brutally murdered on a cross by people trained in execution. Make no mistake, after a Roman crucifixion there was no doubt that the crucified was dead.

Therefore, Jesus' own claims to deity, that He and God were one (John 10:30), were given confirming evidence by the power exhibited in His own resurrection.

When we recognize the deity of Jesus the Messiah, because of His resurrection, then we can recognize that Jesus, as God, used the Old Testament of the Bible as an authoritative source in teaching and instruction while on Earth. Jesus would regularly reference Old Testament Scripture, and even alluded to Adam and Eve (Matthew 19:4-5) when teaching and correcting His disciples and His opponents.

God recognizes no higher authority than himself. This means the Old Testament carries divine authorship. Therefore, its contents have an instructive authority over us.

Then, Jesus, the divine inspiration behind the Old Testament (for He and the Father are one), gave instruction to the apostles to spread His name to all nations (Matthew 28:19-20). This instruction led to the further recording of His story in the form of the New Testament. Therefore, we understand that we can depend upon the New Testament with the same level of trustworthiness as the Old Testament. For the people given the authority to write it were given that authority from God himself, the same author of the authoritative Old Testament.

Once we know that we can trust the New Testament, this gives us a completed revelation from God in the form of the Bible in which we have the true and accurate history of the entire universe starting with the literal 6-day creation. The Bible gives us the history of the universe including the remaining prophetic times that have yet to come. The biggest of which is the return of our glorious King.

Ironically, the return of Messiah in triumph is usually referred to by the secular societies as a negative apocalypse. But to the believer the return of Messiah is the beginning of the new eternal kingdom where there is no sin, no suffering, no hardship or tears. It is a beautiful existence where man is fully restored to the image of God, bearing no stamp of the fallen nature that we must now temporarily endure.

Furthermore, the biblical narrative explains that there is no other God, but that there is an active adversary who aims to deceive mankind. Therefore, if the resurrection is in fact true, then all other religions that do not hold to the truth that Jesus is the only way, truth, and life are, by default, false religions. Other religions must be products of the deceiver in an effort to prohibit people from seeing the singular and exclusive truth that Jesus, the Jewish Messiah, is the Alpha and the Omega, the first and the last, the beginning and the end (Revelation 22:13).

The Bible itself is a shining work of deductive reasoning. The Bible sets up the premise of the resurrection, and then deduces the preeminence of Christ as Savior alone, and God alone from that event.

And the complete nature of the Bible is wonderful. The Bible begins with day one of Creation in Genesis 1:1. It then finishes with the promise of the consummation of the everlasting Kingdom by the Lord declaring that He is coming soon (Revelation 22:20). It is a completed record of all creation and humanity. It's quite extraordinary.

Yet, it all rises and falls on the truthfulness of the premise of the resurrection, for that was the ultimate display of divine power that was left as evidence for the world to see so that the correct deductions of the truthfulness of the entire Bible could then be made.

This dependency on the resurrection being true is admitted in the Bible itself.

> And if Christ has not been raised, your faith is futile and you are still in your sins. . . .we are of all people most to be pitied. (1 Corinthians 15:17-19)

How remarkable that the Bible hand-delivered to us the making or breaking point for its entire worldview. Showing an outstanding confidence, the Bible gave us a manner in which to render the faith built upon it null and void, or to recognize its divine supremacy. Such a display is not a sign of a myth that is weak and feeble. It is a demonstration of strength and ultimate assuredness.

No other worldview delivers such a singular statement in which all rises and falls. No other worldview is as complete and well-reasoned as the biblical worldview. Christianity (Messianic Judaism), the belief that Jesus (Yeshua), was the prophesied Jewish Messiah, of the House of David, who brings salvation to the entire world for anyone who repents of their sin and believes in Him, is truly an ironclad case based on His crucifixion and resurrection. How beautiful this is for us. For this is exactly where we should expect it to rest, on the person of Jesus the Messiah and His supreme claim of deity.

> It may assist the reader in estimating the value of this argument, to consider upon how different a footing, in this respect, has rested every other religious system, without exception, which was ever proposed to the world; and, indeed, every other historical fact, of which the truth has been at all contested.

Dear reader, it is impossible to overestimate the excellence of true Christianity—the Christianity of our Lord Jesus Christ.[13]

—William Wilberforce

13  William Wilberforce , *William Wilberforce–Greatest Works,* Bridge-Logos, 2007, pg. 122

# CHAPTER ELEVEN

# YOU CAN'T FIGHT SCIENCE

◆ ◆ ◆

You are not to be dogmatical in theology, my brethren . . . but for scientific men it is the correct thing. You are never to assert anything very strongly; but scientists may boldly assert what they cannot prove, and may demand a faith far more credulous than any we possess. Forsooth, you and I are to take our Bibles and shape and mold our belief according to the ever-shifting teachings of so-called scientific men.

What folly is this! Why, the march of science, falsely so called, through the world may be traced by exploded fallacies and abandoned theories. Former explorers once adored are now ridiculed; the continual wreckings of false hypotheses is a matter of universal notoriety. You may tell where the learned have encamped by the debris left behind of suppositions and theories as plentiful as broken bottles. (C.H. Spurgeon, *The Sword and the Trowel,* 1877, pg. 197)

We have seen the excellence of the Bible. We have witnessed the brilliance in its composition. We know how the Lord gave us a mind of reason to readily perceive His existence and then to grow in this blessed faith daily.

But then there is the other side—the side of secularism; the side of scoffers; the side of Pontius Pilate who still asks, "What is truth?"

As Bible believers we must be proactive to protect our minds and to equip our spirits. We do this so that we understand the deceptions of our adversary.

This decidedly secular worldview is built on foundations of far less sturdy material than the Bible. In recent centuries, the secular worldview has hijacked science. Science, which should be a good thing, has morphed in the halls of academia, into something beyond real science. It has become the cornerstone of a secular religion.

We have all heard the "you can't fight science" declaration. This movement has sadly caused a widespread exodus of many Christians from fundamental doctrines. Preachers, teachers, and seminaries have abandoned a straightforward reading of Genesis, among other Scriptures. They have renounced such biblical staples as a six-day creation and a worldwide flood because men with degrees in science who have asserted their conclusions about nature are to be trusted more than the history found in the Bible.

Biblical ignorance has caused Christians to fall to these claims, but this faintness of heart is tragic and unnecessary! Why do we think *science* is so strong? Is it the constant chatter that we hear from the secular world that elevates science to that mystical level? Is it because we are being told that scientists do not have bias or agendas, but are rather pure and virtuous and their answers are based only on what the data suggests? Why do we pretend that scientists have somehow been excused from being recipients of the original sin of Adam?

One answer to why Christians bend their faith to appease secular ideas is that we've forgotten the spirit of David charging Goliath. We refuse to go to the river and gather our stones.

For reasons lost to me, Christians earnestly pine for validation from the secular population. Let's not forget that the righteousness of Christ never seeks the approval of the world. We offer illumination; we do not dim our lamps.

This search for worldly approval has left Christians weaponless in the fight against advancing secularism. Through the worldly pressures we have allowed science to stand on a higher pedestal than the Bible itself. In ignorance we have traded the divine Word of God for the conclusions of fallible man.

In our weakness we have allowed science to be the measure of all knowledge systems. This faulty philosophical position places man as the governor of the Bible instead of the Bible issuing its governance to man.

Because we have been swept away in this swell, I believe it is high time that we take a critical look at exactly what *science* is. For it is of no surprise that the scientists rarely discuss or even admit the natural limitations of their disciplines.

The whole premise of science, which finds its roots in the sampling of some data so that conclusions can be drawn on a broader scale, is the modeled practice of *inductive reasoning*—which, of course, is logically fallacious.

I am guessing that most do not realize the practice of science is inductive and fallacious by its nature. This fact is not something that is highly advertised because many scientists, who push a secular worldview, often position themselves as the suppliers of ultimate truth. If they marketed their own weakness it would be damaging to the idea that they, through science, can provide all the answers.

However, whenever a device is used that is known to cause uncertainty in its conclusions, then it is not appropriate to make unwavering statements of absolute truth using such a method.

Now, let's be clear here, answers can still be true that come from inductive reasoning, but the only way to confirm them is by using an outside confirming source. Induction, by its nature, cannot give absolute answers.

And there is the rub. Secular philosophies claim that through science alone absolute certainty can be reached. Yet, because science, at its core, is inductive, it prevents absolute certainty from being reached.

For every tool, there is a proper application—and an improper application, a perfect use, and an imperfect one. Science is a very powerful tool. In fact, its mere practice is a demonstrable proof that mankind *is* unique from the animal kingdom.

We alone sit atop the hill of scientific inquiry. Only mankind, of all beings in existence, practices science. Science is the gathering of data, so conclusions can be attempted. But animals do not practice

139

science because they do not have cognitive ability. God does not practice science because He has no need to gather data, for He is already omniscient. Therefore, science is uniquely human, and though it exalts mankind above the animal kingdom it clearly humbles us below God.

Before one believes that I am simply a Bible man trying to score cheap points against scientists, consider the words of scientist Dr. Jonathan Sarfati:

> There's also this idea of inductive arguments . . . which is actually a fallacy and in fact science is inductive and therefore it's logically fallacious. It doesn't mean that it's not useful. It's very useful . . . I'm a scientist myself. But still it is logically fallacious.[14]

Some scientists do have a proper perspective and have no problem admitting the

14  Dr. Jonathan Sarfati, *Leaving Your Brains At the Church Door?*, Creation Publishers

limitations of their discipline.

It may surprise some that Charles Darwin's entire hypothesis of evolution can be a case study in using inductive reasoning to the extreme extent and failing to catch the errors due to it.

Charles Darwin recognized that animals had different variations within their species. In the case of finches, different finches on different islands had different sized beaks from their cousins on other islands. The size and type of beak seemed to correspond with the kind of seed the finch fed upon on each island. Creationists understand this change and variation within the kinds to be partly a result of Natural Selection, and partly due to a design within the original kinds. And, in fact, Edward Blythe, a creationist, published his work on Natural Selection years before Darwin did.

What Darwin did is that he took the idea of the small variation that could be observed in animal kinds (like the different beaks) and then made a broad sweeping conclusion, which is the inductive reasoning model. Viewing the small changes within creatures like the finches, he then concluded that he could see no limit to the amount of change that natural selection could produce. Thus, this was his generalized theory of evolution.

He took a very small particle, and then he made an enormously far-reaching conclusion. The *no limit* part was and is the logical fallacy, and this was his error. Unfortunately, Darwin had more lapses in judgment.

His conclusion was so far reaching that he uncritically accepted millions and millions of years of past unknown history into it as well. He believed that if there was no limit to the amount of change, and if millions and millions of years were added to the story, then microbes could evolve into men. Darwin's conclusion remains, to this day, one of the largest logical fallacies that man has committed, and our entire society is paying for it.

He not only used inductive reasoning, which is logically fallacious, but his inductive reasoning led to a conclusion (no limits), that had never been seen, and the proof of his conclusion, which had never been seen, was then said to have happened in the distant past where no one could ever go.

This reckless beginning for the conjecture of evolution became engrained in the science of evolution from that point on. Here are some examples of how evolutionary scientists built upon the poor model begun by Darwin.

Fragments of fossils are often excavated and collected for study. Evolutionary-minded scientists employ artists armed with paintbrushes to produce elaborate pictures of entire creatures, complete with skin, eyes, and hair, from just the fragments of fossils that they find. They are masters at creating the illusion of reality. Notwithstanding, this is inductive reasoning in action with no boundaries to catch the errors.

Just one example is found in *Nebraska Man*. Nebraska Man was said to be the ever-elusive missing link in man's evolution. From a tiny find, a most complete model of a creature was invented. However, only a single tooth was ever found, and from that one tooth, an entire image of Nebraska Man was rendered.

The rendering of Nebraska man looked like a physical cross between a man and an ape.

This is inductive reasoning put into practice where no restraints were used to curb the wild conjecture. The average person would reason that this was a reckless use of a tooth. The problem was compounded years later when that tooth was found to be the tooth of a pig.

It took nearly a decade for Nebraska Man to get retracted as a missing link. More interestingly, the retraction, which took years, is now cited as an example of evolutionary science correcting itself. But this explanation fails, because in the correction, they never doubt their theory, nor the methods that led to the forgery. And, certainly, they never were able to correct all the people who were deceived.

A more recent example is the chimp-like creature named Lucy.

Even though the evidence did not support it, artists added some human-like features to the face of Lucy and put human-like feet on her. They used inductive reasoning to whimsically fill in the large gaps that their evidence did not provide. In doing so, they created a misleading image of this creature.

Another example was written about on May 19th, 1994, in the *Sydney Morning Herald*. The newspaper wrote that a discovery of a European fossil named *Boxgrove Man* was, "One of the most important finds in the history of human evolution."

Well, this discovery must certainly be an overwhelming piece of evidence to be labeled with such grandeur. The artist's illustration of Boxgrove Man showed a robust individual with broad shoulders, an upright stance in the hips and spine (like humans), hair on top of the head, deep inquisitive eyes, and facial hair.

However, it also had a longer jawbone and some ape-like features in the nose and mouth. Therefore, this is a classic intermediate creature between man and ape. The paper also reported that Boxgrove Man liked to eat elephants.

This may surprise some to learn that all that was found of Boxgrove Man was a chunk of shinbone approximately eight inches long and a couple of teeth. This is inductive reasoning in practice with an unbridled bias for the hypothesis of evolution.

Yet, what happens? It is the artists drawing and story of eating elephants that gets circulated as fact. But the only fact is that a few fragments of the creature were found. Even so, it was paraded as a missing link of evolution.

This is the danger of inductive reasoning when no authority is recognized to govern it. It leads to conclusions that bias finds, regardless if the evidence supports the conclusion. Yet, this is where much of secular science resides when it tries to redefine human origins.

As Bible believers, we need to be equipped enough to filter the information that we are being fed. We need to understand that so much of our information that is being given to us is from secular-minded people who believe science is the only measure by which we can accumulate knowledge and measure truth. These same people reject the history given to us in the Bible. And because of the original sin of Adam, these people are warring against God, whether they know it or not, and too often we accept their information uncritically.

The bottom line is that science is inductive and, therefore, it cannot be the end-all answer to everything. Ultimate truth can only be ascertained when all the data is known. However, science exists for precisely the opposite reason—not all the natural data is known. Therefore, a complete and isolated reliance on man's science consigns us to an eternal grade of incomplete in the discovery of ultimate answers.

But the people who perpetuate their secular worldview hide the fact that their science has inherent shortcomings. The biblical body, above all, should have discerned this years ago. Science in its pure form is very useful. But it is most useful when it is governed by the truth found in the Bible.

It is for this reason that the Bible, which is a generalized statement of truth by which deductions can be safely made, is the governor of inductive conclusions. When man's science arrives at a conclusion that is contrary to the Bible (like putting human feet on Lucy and making ape-men out of a pig's tooth) then it is man that must determine what error was made in their inductive reasoning.

It is never the correct answer to change what the Bible states to match the most recent claim of science. The Bible molds our view of reality and judges the conclusions of our science. This is why the Bible is not a science book. It is far greater than that.

We can and should use scientific exploration, but let's not ascribe a power to it that it does not deserve. It is not the all-encompassing measure of knowledge. Far from it! It can't be because of its inductive base. It is a useful tool as long as we keep its application within the correct parameters and limits.

The Bible is and will forever be the governor of science and not vice-versa. But as long as we grant science a seat above the Bible, we will be limiting our mind to only seeing mere slices of creation, and, consequently, missing out on the Creator.

# CHAPTER TWELVE

# IN THE BEGINNING, ALIEN?

• • •

As we all know people do put man's conclusions above the truth in the Bible. People lust after their own glory, and spurn the authority of God. In America, we have allowed God to be removed from the public square and from the halls of instruction. As that slide began, many strong believers knew that there would be severe consequences, and there have been. The object now is to stop sowing the bitter seeds.

Bible believers have a moral mandate to be lights to our cultures, but that has not happened with enough force. Through the Lord, we have been given all we need to be the voice of reason, but we have failed to claim what was ours and have allowed the abandonment of basic biblical truth in our neighborhoods. This left a void that is readily being filled by foolishness.

People who believe in the God of the Bible should expect that any worldview that begins with the rejection of God would land in utter confusion. The born-again serve a God of order. Therefore, when that order is rejected, only disorder remains. However, God is not to be mocked, and though we have failed to be strong in voice, God is still the Lion of Judah. In His perfect timing, He will expose the follies that we have allowed to come to pass.

I believe we are nearing the apex of such with those who ascribe to the philosophies of Postmodern Progressivism.

For many years those who rejected God as the Creator held to a belief that life spontaneously created itself out of the primordial soup some 3.5 billion years ago. Out of a random disorder they believe complex order arose. Out of chaos, they believe natural laws were established.

In order to believe this kind of story, these people had to believe in the utmost simplicity of a single cell which, theoretically, would have been numbingly easy to stumble itself into existence. But the Lord has exposed this to be an empty hope.

The cell, as is now understood, is meticulously engineered. It boasts a design far beyond anything humans have even imagined. The molecular biologist, Michael Denton, explains this complexity with descriptive and intriguing language in his book *Evolution: A Theory in Crisis*:

> To grasp the reality of life as it has been revealed by molecular biology, we must magnify a cell a thousand millions times until it is twenty kilometers in diameter and resembles a giant airship large enough to cover a great city like London or New York. What we would then see would be an object of unparalleled complexity and adaptive design. On the surface of the cell we would see millions of openings, like the port holes of a vast space ship, opening and closing to allow a continual stream of materials to flow in and out. If we were to enter one of these openings we would find ourselves in a world of supreme technology and bewildering complexity.[15]

It is, in fact, impossible that a living cell

---

15    M. Denton, *Evolution: A Theory in Crisis,* Adler and Adler Publishers, Inc., 1986), p. 328

simply created itself through random chemical exertions from a primordial soup. The idea of a very primitive life that would be easy to self-assemble simply has no bearing in reality. And now, even those in the tallest towers of evolutionary belief are wilting under that weight. The idea of spontaneous creation of life on Planet Earth is going extinct among evolutionists.

The Lord has allowed secular science to pin themselves into a cramped corner— for the extraordinary complexity of life demands a Creator. But how does this new concession of a Creator work with materialism that tries to exclude God?

This is where it gets interesting. Both sides that are *in the know* of the creation vs. evolution debate now acknowledge that a definitive author of life is needed that is external, or beyond the confines of earth. This has left mankind with only two options for our origins—"In the beginning, God," *or* In the beginning,

Alien.

For the Bible believer, this realization finds us comfortably reclining on the divine mountaintop where we have been for thousands of years. We have always known that an external force created us. We have always known that God is, and was, and is to come.

But, for the Postmodern Progressives, they have been forced to abandon what their science has told them yet again. And now they are climbing Mount Unreasonable in search for aliens.

Richard Dawkins, a prominent atheistic and evolutionary propagator admitted on the documentary, "Expelled," that there was an idea gaining ground that aliens seeded life on this planet.

Dawkins is not the first to bring this to light, and we are seeing an overwhelming trend of evolutionary scientists being beamed aboard this ship. Sir Francis Crick is a figure that has been instrumental in this doctrine of alien forefathers. He had this to say:

> An honest man, armed with all the knowledge available to us now, could only state that in some sense, the origin of life appears at the moment to be almost a miracle, so many are the conditions which would have had to have been satisfied to get it going.[16]

Yet, for Crick, the idea of God creating the heavens and the earth was too big a pill to swallow. Therefore, he pushed an idea of what is commonly called *panspermia.* Under this idea life somehow was generated, accidentally of course, in the deep expanses of the universe. This life then naturally advanced through evolution into highly developed beings. Finally, such alien life somehow traveled to our planet and seeded life here on earth.

---

16    Sir Francis Crick, Quoted in "Panspermia," www. creationdefense.org/68.htm, March 9, 2003.

Thus, the genesis of all life is explained.

However, this naive idea still does not solve the enigma of how life began for the secularist. It only pushes the problem to a place where no one can ever go. One cannot solve a problem by creating a world where the answer is impossible to find. This idea of panspermia is evidence of Satan's victory over the mind of some individuals.

But, as believers, we can't find any pride in this. Not standing firm on the account of Creation, found in Genesis, has led to this nonsense. When we allow the true Creation account found in the Bible to be dismissed, should we not expect that void to be filled in with foolishness?

This delusion that aliens are out there has moved to a belief that visitation has actually happened. Harvard professor John Mack wrote a book called *Abduction: Human Encounters with Aliens.* He believed that aliens have already abducted humans and collected sperm and eggs.

Meanwhile, one of the most heralded of all evolutionary thinkers is the famed Stephen Hawking, and he deemed it necessary to warn us not to talk to alien life-forms that he believes exist. Hawking was quoted in an article entitled, "Don't Talk to Aliens":

> We only have to look at ourselves to see how intelligent life might develop into something we wouldn't want to meet. I imagine they might exist in massive ships, having used up all the resources from their home planet. Such advanced aliens would perhaps become nomads, looking to conquer and colonize whatever planets they can reach.[17]

Did Stephen Hawking just hi-jack the plot of *War of the Worlds* and then try to pass it

---

17 Stephen Hawking, The Sunday Times, "Don't Talk To Aliens, Warns Stephen Hawking," April 25, 2010

off as scientific insight—an exalted secular scientist hopelessly confused between science and science fiction? The humor is lost because the deception is so severe and souls are hanging in the balance.

If you remember from a previous chapter, we discussed that Hawking also believes that our entire universe spontaneously arose out of nothing, which is the prevailing belief of secular academia. This is a massive conundrum for the secular thinker. One must wonder why the simple cell on earth is too complex to create itself, and that it now demands a designer (even though they invoke an unknown alien designer), but then it is okay if the entire universe, which contains all of this complexity, spontaneously pops into existence by accident without a designer? These secular beliefs are tripping over themselves and the inability to make consistent lines of thought is a telltale sign that their worldview of secular philosophies has failed.

If an individual truly decides, after thinking this issue through, that all the matter and symbiotic moving parts within the entire universe is a product of a ball of energy the size of a pinhead that somehow expanded, after it somehow just popped up, then such a person has lost every string of reason that ties a mind together. But this kind of irrational conclusion has become acceptable within the walls of secular science. Take into consideration the words of the Harvard Geneticist, Richard Lewontin, a proponent of evolution:

> Our willingness to accept scientific claims that are against common sense is the key to an understanding of the real struggle between science and the supernatural. We take the side of science in spite of the patent absurdity of some of its constructs, in spite of its failure to fulfill many of its extravagant promises of health and life, in spite of the tolerance of the scientific

community for unsubstantiated just-so stories, because we have a prior commitment, a commitment to materialism. . . . materialism is absolute, for we cannot allow a Divine Foot in the door.[18]

It is of the utmost importance to see the guiding principle in today's secular academic scientists. They cannot, in any way, allow a Divine Foot in the door, an acknowledgment of an all-powerful Creator, to enter any discussion. Thus, when the evidence demands a designer, they are forced to pen their own story that starts with, "In the beginning, Alien." They do this in spite of its patent absurdity. Many of your children are probably being educated and graded by these kinds of people, and you may be incurring financial debt for this to happen.

These conclusions of alien designers are not the extent of the folly. According to

---

18  Richard Lewontin, "Billions and Billions of Demons," New York Review, January 9, 1997, p.31.

the Postmodern Progressive worldview, science, driven by materialism, is the manner in which we can discover truth. If scientists cannot observe it, or prove it, then it does not exist.

But alien life has never been verified. So, according to their own philosophy of materialism, they are treading in a place where they should not be. The secular world ridicules Christians for believing in God for the very reason that He is not seen. Yet, this is where secularists have landed with aliens, and for them it is okay.

Their folly is further exposed because they believe that rather than the life on earth, it is the aliens who are the ones who have now been spontaneously formed out of non-living chemicals. But, the whole idea of any life being created out of non-living chemicals actually breaks the scientific law of biogenesis.

The universally accepted law of biogenesis states that life must come from life.

Of all the scientific observations and accumulation of data, we have never witnessed a single living organism that was created that did not come from another life.

The supposed spontaneous creation of alien life, out of non-living matter, in a galaxy, far, far away, contradicts the law of biogenesis. Therefore, this belief must be considered a blind faith for it has zero evidence backing the claim. Thus, belief in alien life breaks the Postmodern Progressive's own tenets of materialism and science as the measure of all knowledge.

There is yet another problem for the Postmodern Progressive. How life originated free from a God is only one of two enigmas for their anti-God worldview. The other is how did the universe itself come into existence?

Pulling from the earlier quote, Stephen Hawking and Leonard Mlodinow rationalized our beginnings this way:

As recent advances in cosmology suggest, the laws of gravity and quantum theory allow universes to appear *spontaneously from nothing.* Spontaneous creation is the reason there is something rather than nothing, why the universe exists, *why we exist.*[19] (italics added)

But, our entire existence testifies that there is something in existence. The philosophy of materialism does not allow anyone to believe that there ever was a state of nothing. Materialism would make us conclude that there has always been something that existed because that is all that we have ever observed. To believe there ever was utter nothingness is a blind faith not supported by the Postmodern Progressive's own tenets of materialism.

Now, this does not mean that the universe could be eternal. It is not. We know this

19   Stephen Hawking and Leonard Mlodinow, "Why God Did Not Create the Universe," Wall Street Journal, Retrieved on September 9, 2010

because the universe is burning energy while showing no ability to replenish itself. It is like a spinning top winding down. Therefore, according to the secularist's own philosophy of materialism, there must have been something before this universe existed, and something after it ends.

Then according to science, the law of biogenesis states that life must come from life. Therefore, this forces us to conclude, if we hold only to science as our measure for knowledge, that there must be an originator of life, which has always lived because there has to be a first life-form from which life sprung. And that first life-form could not have sprung from non-living chemicals, for this contradicts biogenesis. Therefore, the conclusion that the first life-form always has been is the only conclusion we can make if we abide solely by man's science.

According to man's philosophies of materialism, and the belief that in science all answers are found, we are to conclude that there was an existence of something before this universe existed, and that there is an eternal life force that was the genesis of all other life.

The very philosophies that were meant to allow a belief in atheism actually do the reverse. For these atheistic geared philosophies present an argument, when followed to their logical ends, that there must have been something in existence before the present universe and there must be a living being that had no beginning. Life simply was.

It is quite a natural conclusion then that this eternal living being would give us a reasonable explanation to the prior existence of this universe that materialism suggests.

What becomes evident is that the one extraordinary demand that our existence needs is an eternal power that can wield the genesis of all life itself; an all-powerful eternal first cause—a grand organizing designer.

The claims of the God of the Bible match the criteria that materialism and biogenesis would suggest is necessary for our existence. As hard as this can be to fathom, this is the only thing that makes sense to believe.

This leaves us at a fascinating crossroads, for what exactly then is the faith of a Bible believer? What is it that I must believe based on a blessed hope? Because the evidence of God trumps simply having a faith that He merely exists.

My faith is not that God created the universe. It is not that He alone stands as God, an all-powerful Creator who lives eternally, from everlasting to everlasting. Those attributes of God are what the universe and all existence demands Him to be. I believe the evidence demonstrates, with the crack of a sun-sized gavel, that the God of the Bible is the supreme power in existence and He rose from the dead as a testimony to His supremacy over all. I believe that is the evidence that we have.

My step of faith is that this very all powerful Creator God who has the power to wield planets and galaxies, who has the tides rise and recede on His word, who has the trees, mountains, and canyons testify to His greatness, who paints the auroras across the northern skies, and who has the very power to create all of life, that this God actually has an ear that will hear my prayers. That this God of the Bible knows my joys, and He knows all of my trials. He has a heart that desires to be close to mine, and has a grace to bring me out of rebellion, to induce my repentance, so that He can save me from myself and have a relationship of Father and son with me. That is my step of faith, that the Creator of the universe loves me—for that is the biggest miracle of them all.

# CHAPTER THIRTEEN

# SPIRITUAL COMA

◆ ◆ ◆

By acting without thought or reason, we dishonor the God that made us reasonable creatures, we often become injurious to our neighbors, kindred or friends, and we bring sin and misery upon ourselves: for we are accountable to God our judge for every part of our irregular and mistaken conduct, where he hath given us sufficient advantages to guard against those mistakes.[20] (Isaac Watts)

20   Isaac Watts, *The Improvement of the Mind* (Bangs & Mason: NY), 1822, pg.16.

One would expect the secular cauldron of ideas to confuse and mislead the secular world, but not the believer. But, regrettably, such deceptions have ensnared ill-equipped Christians who unwisely follow the usurper's way. And I fully confess that all of us, myself included, are guilty of this in more ways than we would wish to admit.

Remarkably, it is happening when all the evidence should be bolstering faith in Almighty God. And it is not only the laymen that are misled. Our teachers are slipping away. It should be remembered that those who take on the yoke of teaching are held to a different standard.

> Not many of you should become teachers, my brothers, for you know that we who teach will be judged with greater strictness. (James 3:1)

Any who undertake the office to teach, write, and speak should understand the stakes. A careful word tempered by the fear of the Lord is a must. But instead of prudence and caution in speech, some have created, within our circles, a professional pulpit built with pride and recklessness.

An ominous sky has set over the seminaries, professors, and the large mass of all too liberal pastors of our Christian teaching institutions and churches. We have allowed the cancer of Postmodern Progressivism to pervert our views. We have traded the purity of simplicity found in the Bible, for the tangled mess of ambiguity found in the scoffers' remarks.

We will look at only two issues of the nearly infinite number available, of where Postmodern Progressivism is disposing of the believer's spiritual discernment. I chose these two, because they deal with the bookends of our faith—our beginning and our end.

For our first example, there is a clot of commentators within the veins of the modern church who, again, cannot make sense out of the first chapter of Genesis. A chapter so simply written, that it would take a self-induced stroke to find a place of confusion.

Here is a portion of the Genesis text, which seems to cause so much anxiety:

> And God said, "Let the waters swarm with swarms of living creatures, and let birds fly above the earth across the expanse of the heavens." So God created the great sea creatures and every living creature that moves, with which the waters swarm, according to their kinds, and every winged bird according to its kind. And God saw that it was good. And God blessed them, saying, "Be fruitful and multiply and fill the waters in the seas, and let birds multiply on the earth." And there was evening and there was morning, the fifth day. (Genesis 1:20-23)

There are those who claim to be within the circle of Bible believers who *interpret* this passage as meaning nothing that is written.

It has and is being claimed that this entire creation account is just an artistic metaphor. To some, the *fifth day* does not mean a real fifth day, and *morning and evening* do not mean a real morning and evening; and *according to their kinds* does not mean according to their kinds. Indeed, to some, the entire first chapter of Genesis, which details how God created the heavens and the earth, has merely become a story that is no longer instructing us on how God created the heavens and the earth!

The reason why people try to ignore a literal reading of Genesis is that the biblical creation account is in stark contradiction to the Big Bang idea hailing from the secular scientists. However, as we pointed out earlier, the Big Bang does not stand on a foundation that either rationale or real science can build. Yet, Christians are foregoing the deductive genius of the Bible, and its creation account, for the whimsical ideas of secular man.

Postmodern Progressives have found willing theologians who will vacate the truth, wisdom, and soundness of divine Scripture. They have successfully used those *of the cloth* to publicly argue that man's science should be the governor of the Bible.

However, this idea that the creation account of Genesis is a mere parable, with no bearing in reality, fails very quickly with a biblical cross check. In the book of Exodus, one of the pillars of our faith is found in chapter twenty, which contains the Ten Commandments.

Of the Ten Commandments, the fourth commandment is to keep the Sabbath Holy. The Sabbath was predicated on one act alone. It is to remember the seventh day of rest after the Lord's six-day creation.

For in six days the LORD made heaven and earth, the sea, and all that is in them, and rested on the seventh day. Therefore the LORD blessed the Sabbath day and made it holy. (Exodus 20:11)

This is why the six-day creation account is not only mentioned in Genesis—but is a tenet in the Ten Commandments: the Creation account explains when sin entered the world (Genesis 3). The Law was given in order for people to recognize their own depravity, which arose with the sin of Adam. Without the understanding of our perfect, sinless, beginning, and then the introduction of sin into the world at the hands of Adam, we would not understand why we were given the Ten Commandments.

Therefore, we would expect one of the Ten Commandments to be built around the Creation account. It was imperative that God explained to us the unbreakable tie between the first week of Creation, when all was perfect, and then the subsequent fall of man that brought evil, sin, disease, and suffering to the previously "good" creation. And it was such an important theme, that the Lord commanded all generations to remember the Sabbath and to keep it holy.

In the New Testament, the Sabbath and the truth of Creation is shown again. Hebrews 4:10 reads:

> (F)or whoever has entered God's rest has also rested from his works as God did from his.

Biblical wisdom teaches that Genesis was not a parable, but a very real account of the actions of God. And the Creation week was important enough for the Lord God to base a commandment of remembrance upon it.

Yet, to rework Genesis 1, to the extent that nothing is as it seems, destroys this thread of continuity, which was divinely woven.

Once the Creation account is dismissed as real history, a stress fracture spreads like a crack in a windshield over other parts of Scripture. For every New Testament author quotes or alludes to Genesis and many of the references are speaking of the first three chapters.

And if one rejects our foundations in Genesis, soon much of the Bible becomes confusing because the anchor of the ship is removed and waves are free to cast the ship to and fro.

The Bible is not an à la carte menu where we can choose what we want to believe. It is one continuous spiritual feed that works together. These people who reject our foundation automatically lose the majesty of seeing the inspired unity of the greatest book ever written. Consequently, their faith, their walk, and their Christian witness suffer dramatically, which has eternal ramifications.

However, we, influenced by secular ideas, do pick and choose what is real and what is not. I offer a case in point with a statement from Dr. James Montgomery Boice. In this statement, he is speaking of the relatively young timeline of the history of the earth when a literal six-day creation week is applied to our history instead of invoking the billions of years that the secular evolutionists need for their model of origins (the term *creationist,* in this context, is referring to those who believe in the literal six-day creation).

We have to admit here that the exegetical basis of the creationists is strong . . . In spite of the careful biblical and scientific research that has accumulated in support of the creationists' view, there are problems that make the theory wrong to most (including many evangelical) scientists . . . Data from various disciplines point to a very

old earth and an even older universe
. . . If the earth and the universe look
old when they actually are not, why
should any of our observations be
trusted?[21]

Immediately, Dr. Boice admits that the clear reading of the Genesis creation account is on the side of the creationists. This is what he means when he admitted the "exegetical basis of the creationists is strong." But by the end of the statement, he discarded what the biblical text clearly stated in favor of human *observations*. But, here is the conflict—no one alive *observed* the creation. Do we have ability to put God in the wrong and condemn His Word so that we can be in the right on an account that we have never seen?

Where were we when God laid the foundations of the earth?

---

21  Dr. James Montgomery Boice, Pastor, (speaker on The Bible Study Hour), Genesis, An Expositional Commentary, Vol. 1, pages 56-62.

Have any of us commanded the morning since the days began and caused the dawn to know its place?

Did mere man establish the ordinances of the heavens; did we establish the laws of nature that issue their governance to us?

Is it at our command that the eagle mounts up and makes his nest on high?

Do we have an arm like God and can we thunder with a voice like His? Can we allow our own death and then rise three days later?

If only man would find a knee to bow and answer like Job when addressed with these kinds of questions!

> Therefore I have uttered what I did not understand, things too wonderful for me, which I did not know. . . . therefore I despise myself, and repent in dust and ashes. (Job 42:3, 6)

Our spiritual coma is our immense pride that we have the ability to establish our own truth and make a mere cut and paste collage of what we want the Bible to say.

This brings us to example number two of the effects of Postmodern Progressivism on Theology. With that, I should clarify what theology is. Theology is the study of any kind of deity in which someone believes. It can refer to the study of the God of the Bible, but it is not restricted to that. Therefore, those who call themselves theologians are not necessarily followers of Jesus the Messiah.

In some cases, a born-again Bible believer is separated by a huge expanse from the so-called theologian. Sadly, more often than not, the *biblical* theology taught in seminaries is a cold, barren gulf of liberalism that the born-again believer wants nothing to do with. It would be wise to take note that the greatest deception achieves such deceit from within.

Dr. William Crockett is a professor of New Testament at Alliance Theological Seminary. In one of his published works, he outlines a very aggressive argument about the doctrine of eternal punishment, the place of hell.

Hell is something that nearly the entire world holds some concept of—even those who never darken the door of a church understand that hell is synonymous with a place filled with fire. The Bible does not mix words about this. A fiery hell is a consistent reality throughout the New Testament.

> It is better for you to enter life crippled than with two hands to go to hell, to the unquenchable fire. (Mark 9:43)

> But as for the cowardly, the faithless, the detestable, as for murderers, the sexually immoral, sorcerers, idolaters, and all liars, their portion will be in the lake that burns with

fire and sulfur, which is the second death." (Revelation 21:8)

Those who are not born again, who do not repent of their sins and ask for the saving substitute of Jesus the Messiah, which was made possible through His crucifixion and His resurrection, remain guilty of their sins, which will forever separate them from an almighty and perfect God. The Bible is clear that those people go to hell. Hell is as certain as every other doctrine of the Bible if the axiom of the resurrection of Jesus is true.

The idea that hell is a fiery place is an open and shut case, right? But what can occur when someone, influenced by Postmodern Progressivism, simply does not like the idea of a fiery hell?

Despite the overwhelming imagery matching fire with hell, Dr. Crocket contended that hell is not filled with fire at all. His position is that the multiple verses that consistently speak of hell as being a place of fire are only meant to express that hell is a place we do not want to go.

Crockett exhibited the traits of a Postmodern Progressive—the intent of the author is thrown aside for the wishes of the reader.

But why would Crockett attempt redefining what is plain to all? In the previous scenario with Boice, he felt embarrassed that secular science differed with the Bible. Likewise, the Bible-teacher Crockett is embarrassed about the Bible and its doctrines. Crockett wrote:

> Many in Christendom are repulsed by the message that God will consign part of His creation to a lake of fire. . . . And what happens? We hold our tongues in embarrassment, never mentioning that God will banish the wicked from His presence.[22]

---

22   William Crocket, *Four Views on Hell*, Zondervan, 1996, pg. 54

Allow me to join the million-strong chorus in response to this most regrettable comment. I am not ashamed of the Gospel of Jesus Christ, for it is the power of salvation to all who believe, and that salvation is so named because it is a saving from that very fiery hell.

Since Crockett is embarrassed about the Bible and repulsed at God's message, and, in my opinion, Postmodern Progressivism influences him, he decided that all the imagery of hell being a pit of fire is simply colorful language.

Crockett, as a proof for a non-fiery hell, points out that there are a couple of verses in the Bible that describe hell as a place of gloomy darkness and as an outer darkness (Matthew 8:12, Jude 1:6). Therefore, the Bible creates a composite image of hell being a lake of fire and a place of darkness. Using this information, Crockett advanced the idea that the whole concept of hell being a literal place of eternal fire fails because as he states:

The blackest darkness is hardly compatible with a vast lake of fire.[23]

Crockett concludes that fire could not co-exist in a place that was also described as utter darkness. He argues the two are mutually exclusive. So in one fell swoop, Crockett believed he forced all Bible believers to redefine their view of hell, and thanks to him, we no longer allow the idea of hell to embarrass us:

Christians should never be faced with this kind of embarrassment . . . the Bible does not support a literal view of a burning abyss.[24]

Essentially, the line of reasoning that Crockett used was this: *All fire emits light. Hell is a place of darkness. Therefore, hell cannot be made of fire.*

But, one would ask: Are the axioms true? Has Crockett seen all fires?

23   ibid, page 60
24   ibid, pg. 44

Crockett has not seen all the fires that have ever burned; he has only seen a sample. He then, evidently applied his knowledge of the sample, and made a broad conclusion about the whole. So Crockett attempted to make a logical deduction, but a problem arose because one of his antecedents was derived from inductive reasoning. We know that inductive reasoning is prone to mistakes.

And the Bible, which Crocket should have used to govern his inductive decisions, was disregarded because it was repulsive and embarrassing to him. Crocket applied his inductive reasoning to how he viewed the Biblical text and he tried to force a change in the understanding of eternal punishment.

That is not a good combination. What Crockett should have done first, is ask himself: "Does all fire emit light?"

The answer to that question is, no. Not all fire emits light that the human eye can see.

Crockett's axiom that all fire emits light was not true.

Some extremely hot fires, like some hydrogen fires, are invisible to us. At the John C. Stennis Space Center in Mississippi, NASA worked to develop special lenses, cameras, and imaging techniques to see invisible flames. Such technology was needed as a safety precaution as they work with experimental rockets that have fuels that burn completely and clearly. NASA decided that having an undetected invisible fire raging around rockets and rocket fuel was problematic.[25]

There *are* fires that produce flames that do *not* emit light. Therefore, it is possible that darkness can be in concert with unquenchable flames, after all.

Crockett failed to use the authority of Scripture to govern his own inductive reasoning, and he produced an unsound

---

25   Ruth A. Mondonsa, "Camera Catches Invisible Fires," Photonics Spectra, February 1998

answer. Crockett, though a professing Christian, was acting like a Postmodern Progressive. This Bible teacher provided a seed of sin in a fertile field in his mind. Sin was then cultivated and fed to the point that he wrote in a published work that God was embarrassing and repulsive in His message on eternal punishment.

Also consider that in the first century A.D, when the New Testament was written, it is doubtful those scribes had natural knowledge of invisible flames. The fact that the descriptions of hell, written approximately two millennia ago can be understood by today's standards offers a sobering proof of a literal description of a very real fiery hell where darkness and fire coexist.

Christians, we must condition our minds to seek discernment, to long for the treasures of wisdom, to bow the knee of humility to that in which we do not understand. We must give the God of the universe the proper credit that He is more knowledgeable than we are.

# CHAPTER FOURTEEN

# GRANT ME
# MY DESIRES

◆ ◆ ◆

God chose the most personal, quiet, and intimate way to speak to us. The written Word was developed so that the Great Author himself could directly communicate to each of us individually. And then, in a method known only to the God of the Bible, the Holy Spirit illuminates the mind of the individual reading the Word. He teaches, instructs, and loves His children into growth.

For this reason, the adversary advanced an attack on our minds and the manner in which our minds communicate. If Satan can disable and confuse our minds about the very meaning of a message, then instead of the Bible being God's communication to us, it becomes whatever we wish it to be. The end result is the destruction of our spiritual wisdom and discernment.

Satan's attack did not relent with the postmodern confusion of language. Once the mind was emptied of relevant thought, he sought to fill it with generic junk. Images, noises, the intellectual congestion of media is pressing and attacking every moment of consciousness that we have. Just living today in the western world is an assault on our senses.

There is a strategic attempt to commandeer every last minute of our every day. I found this disturbing statistic that illustrates this: *According to Nielsen, the average American watches more than 143 hours of TV a month.*[26]

26 http://www.foxnews.com/scitech/2011/04/09/tv-finds-killer-app-ipad-tablet/#ixzz1J1yKrUxe

That is almost 5 hours per day of secular inputs, via the television, for the average person in the U.S. That is mind boggling.

We allow the race of the world to keep us so busy, and then when we do eventually rest, we merely vegetate and allow the world to pour into our mind their social agendas. We allow ourselves to get exhausted by baseless engagement throughout the day, and then we relax in a bed of aimlessness.

When someone finally does reach for the Bible, Postmodern Progressivism has sunk so deep, that we believe it is our own right to take from the Bible what we choose instead of studying to learn the intent of the Author. So what is it that we can do? How can the tide be turned back from its surge?

Each of us needs to chase after God with urgency, fervency, and a consuming desire. We need to realize that to not be overwhelmed with the things of God is to not be interested in Him at all. We have to be able to shed the scaly skin of postmodern progressivism and humbly bow before God and admit that our own goals, our own achievements, our own desires are forever put on the back shelf as we pursue the things of God. We have to realize that the goals He has for us, are far greater than any goal we could set up for ourselves. We have to trust Him in this.

A number of years ago, I had the thought that as a born-again believer God would grant me the desires of my heart, as a long as they were not sinful and harmful to me. So I began to think of what it was I should ask for under this premise.

I paged through the Bible and studied Moses, David, and Paul, and I assembled the character traits I desired for myself. It was quite the impressive list. I figured there was no way I could steer myself wrong for I was drawing from stalwarts of the faith.

Yet, when even asking for the venerable traits of some of the most powerful characters in the Bible, I was not acting with true spiritual wisdom and discernment. I was actually using the wisdom of man, the wisdom of me, which was influenced by Postmodern Progressivism.

Because behind those requests was a pride that is very difficult to recognize. It is the most deceptive and concealed pride that we have. It goes back to the very beginning with Adam, and he passed this sin down to all of us and it has been fanned into flame by our adversary ever since. Do you know what my sin of pride was in asking for those honorable and cherished traits that those biblical men demonstrated?

It was this: I believed I knew what was best for me. Regardless of what those traits are, it was arrogant and naïve for me to think that I knew what was best for me in my service to God.

I did not create myself. I do not know how long I will live. I do not know the hairs on my head, the days in my life, the future blessings and struggles that I will have. Therefore, how could I even know what character traits would be the most useful for me?

The fact is, God created all of us for a unique purpose that He alone knows. In my life, my purpose is being revealed to me on a need to know basis. Each day, we walk forward giving that day the strongest effort. No man is promised tomorrow. This is why we ask for our *daily* bread and not our retirement bread.

Therefore, with this small thread of spiritual discernment, God allowed me to understand that the most important desires for me to have, were desires that I did not even know to have. I realized how out of control I really was.

So my prayer became this, "Lord, please give me the desires that you would wish for me to have, and then please grant me those desires, whatever they may be."

It is a prayer free of all Postmodern Progressive infected thought. It is the opposite of us defining our own truth. It is the full submission that God decides who and what we are. Whatever He sees fit for us is what is fit for us. It is a complete surrender where we ask for fulfillment in whatever He wishes us to be fulfilled with—it is death to self, to gain true life in Christ.

After some time, my desires started to change and a new desire in me arose to have a longing to see the world with eternal eyes. I began to desire to see this present world through the perspective of His eternal plan.

It is a desire that I would have never had known to ask for if I had stuck to my own list. But it has been a far greater desire to have than any of the self-propping desires that I once had and felt unashamed to ask for. What desires are you missing out on because you are trying to define your own?

As of my desire to see more clearly, I am sure only the smallest fraction can I understand now. But what I believe I can say is that the blessed remnant will have true greatness thrust upon them in the Kingdom, but God alone is the greatest by an order of magnitude that cannot be measured.

We shall have crowns, but we will lay them back at His feet. We shall have an honorable name, but His name is the Most High. We shall be loved, but He will be loved the most, for He is the most deserving to be loved. His Lordship will be known throughout all the ages, and every living being from every existence will fully understand that truth, even those who are cast away from His presence.

We will stand in perfect wisdom, understanding, and knowledge because we will stand with a strength that will not be our own. And we will be royalty, for we will be made eternally in His perfect image. But even still, we remain the Petros, and He is the Petra. We are a piece of rock, and He is the *mass of rock* and there is none greater.